〈歡樂飲酒歌〉 國際侵權訴訟案

——台灣原住民 vs. 亞特蘭大奧運

蘭天律師 著

目錄

記我與黃秀蘭律師相識的機緣

李道明

二○一七年十月透過老朋友王耿瑜小姐的介紹，我邀請到黃秀蘭律師來當時我所任教的國立臺北藝術大學電影創作學系演講，向大學三、四年級同學說明智慧財產權與電影授權（Intellectual Property & Licensing）、電影相關合約簽訂與注意事項（Signing Contract and Avoiding the Traps）、影視工作者的保險（Insurance for Filmmakers and Production）等議題。這件事的緣起是因為電影創作學系的同學對於智財權──尤其是如何取得授權、如何不違法、如何保護自己的作品（劇本或完成的影片）不被盜用、演員或編導簽合約時應該注意什麼以及如何避免落入陷阱等議題──頗感疑惑，且特別關心。

由於北藝大地處台北市的郊區關渡的山丘上，電影創作學系又位於北藝大的邊疆地帶，所以演講當天我與黃律師約定在北捷關渡站門口接她上山。記得當時我在前門等候多時卻一直沒等到，正在門口四處踱步張望搜尋時，一位盛裝打扮、衣著時髦的熟齡女子突然問我是否是李主任。我猛然意識到她就是黃律師，但她卻與我印象中應該裝扮較為保守的律師形象完全不同。我趕緊邀她上車到學校演講。

由於黃律師的演講深入淺出、面面俱到，讓同學們獲益良多且非常受用，因此當時身為系主任的我就決定自一〇六學年第二學期起聘請黃秀蘭律師來電影創作學系碩士班講授「智慧財產權與合約談判」課程。自此之後，這門課就成了北藝大電影創作學系最受學生歡迎的一門課。黃律師果然不改其律師本色，不但對每週上課的課題仔細安排，更鉅細靡遺地準備各種案例讓同學能既深入且廣泛地了解關於影視工作智慧財產權與合約談判相關的各個層面。更加難能可貴的是，黃律師充分準備的每一堂課的內容，她也毫不藏私地定期公布在她個人的「臉書」網站上，嘉惠所有想獲取影視領域智財權與合約相關知識的業內與業外人士。

黃律師這種將其專業知識無私奉獻給社會的精神，也在這一篇關於EMI唱片公司發行的專輯唱片中引用郭英男夫婦演唱阿美族傳統歌曲〈歡樂飲酒歌〉所引發的一件「侵權國際訴訟案」的專書中具體表現出來。

閱讀這篇文章時，我感覺其精采的程度不下於觀看一本推理小說。我發現黃律師在處理這件相關事件發展歷時數十年的法律訴訟案件時，所經歷的過程正如同一名偵探試圖找尋所有線索、蒐集完整的證據、釐清事件的發展過程，以發掘真相。但比起偵探更困難的是，她還要協助擬定策略，讓對手可以被定罪或願意屈服。現在的影視戲劇正流行製作所謂的「職人劇」。我覺得關於〈歡樂飲酒歌〉的這件侵權國際訴訟案，其實也蠻適合改編成一齣關於智財權律師的「職人劇」。

謹以此文權充黃律師書稿的序文，紀念我們之間友誼。相信透過本文，讀者們可以理解著作權的保護是如何不容易但卻又是十分重要的。

・本文作者為國立臺北藝術大學電影創作學系名譽教授

文化與律法間的重新思辯

黃亞歷

　　讀完蘭天律師與魔岩唱片為馬蘭部落的郭英男先生爭取著作權的過程，除了對於他們在漫長申訴過程中面對各種法律攻防挑戰時所展現的意志與耐心深感敬佩，也對這起近三十年前的重要國際性智慧財產權侵權案例，相映於當代原住民文化與智慧財產權之間的複雜關係，不禁泛起諸多聯想與思考。

　　在本案訴訟過程中十分引人注目之處，是近三十年前的台灣著作權法在當年仍然不夠全面，並有過於簡化的疑慮，包括坊間社會對某些創作權益挾帶了刻板化的錯誤認知，皆反映出政府當局及社會大眾普遍對於藝術、表演在創作面向的認知是相當局限的。

然而，毋寧說一九九六年事發當時的普羅大眾缺乏著作權意識，即使在當代，面對著作權與藝術創作間的複雜關係，多數人也大多一知半解，遇到問題便感到怯步遲疑，更遑論長期以來執政者和整體社會對於原住民權益的漠視與結構性的壓迫，故郭英男案從一開始在台灣首先面對到的挑戰，現在看來並不令人意外。

在郭英男案中，凸顯了一個相當關鍵的問題，即台灣本身的法律對於此案所涉及的「編曲著作權」及「演唱權」是否賦予了著作權法上的充分保護？這也是本案的國際被告律師不斷想針對台灣的立法缺失，強調台灣法律無法支持本案並給予有效保障的反駁立基點。幸虧，台灣於一九六四、一九八五、一九九〇、一九九二、一九九三的逐年修法陸續填補了每一階段的不足，讓郭英男案在台灣有一層尚可解釋的基礎保護傘，得以與國際律師抗衡，爭取更多層有效的訴訟權。

相較於演唱權，「編曲」所標彰的著作權意識，在原住民部落文化中更顯其特殊意涵，作為台灣的少數族群，由於文化與風俗上的差異，在音樂詮釋上常引起爭論的問題是：長年透過口述流傳的古謠唱誦，能夠算是一種「創作」嗎？如果是，這樣的創作則是進行了具創意性的改編或再創，那麼「改編權」（或編曲權）在一九九六年的國際法律上能夠成立，會是基於什麼樣的理由和條件？

雖然最後本案以調出郭英男數十年前的歌謠，對比於一九九四年的版本，並以兩個版本具八十％以上的差異作為編曲著作權成立的法律判準依據。微妙之處在於，若真的強制以科學方法比對，難道七十五％或七十％以下，就真的不足以被認定其創作的合理性嗎？更何況在音樂的感知上，這些微的差異是以難以被科學化的方法界定的。這樣的情況當然也說明了法律終究是藝術性創作最後一道防備，為維護創作的主體尊嚴，卻需要各種以科學連結律法規範出具極端化的條件，方能形成有效的保障，即使這些方法本身逆反了音樂本身的構造與精神。

而這些法律條件的設定與到位，依靠的是法律專家之間的邏輯鬥智、戰術運用，過程中必然耗盡提告與被告雙方的氣力與資源，對於經濟弱勢的一方，經常是難以參與的遙遠世界。幸得蘭天律師義無反顧的克服各種挑戰，加上郭英男夫婦與魔岩唱片的信任與堅持，以及跨國律師團之間的通力合作，才可能獲得勝訴。此案不僅將台灣的著作權法推向一個不同的新階段，也為台灣原住民部落文化，在國際上爭取到合理合法、應有的尊重。

隨著原住民族群在九〇年代後各項權益的爭取及社運的開展，近十多年來，原住民相關著作權法也進入了不同層次的闡釋與面貌，連帶文化復振與政治資源之間的緊密關係，都逐漸影響了涉及族群符號、圖騰、樂舞、口傳內涵，乃至於種種文化意象的運用及詮釋，產生了具爭議性的討論與激辯，當下這些議題或許仍愈加熱烈分歧，但也或許意味著當事者或參與者皆面臨並選擇了不同的文化實踐方式，未來亦會在各種行動中，開闢出更多元的著作權／專用權（原住民族傳統智慧創作保護條例）理解之可能。

尤以著作權的概念來自於西方法制，如何更有彈性地適切於強調集體意識的部落文化，或需延展出更多的協商、討論機制，方能在強調個體創作性的現代律法中，找到權衡之道。

郭英男國際侵權案作為部落文化著作權發聲的具體實踐，不僅有不容忽視的時代意義，其細節與規範權益的立基點與運用方式，對於當代思考創作與法律設定的關係，提供了值得深思的參照線索。

在傳統循守與當代編創共織於法定規範下的集體族群界分、部落自主意識的法規化、政治化之間，當人們在傳承過往、詮釋新意的同時，如何不被既定的分類框架所束縛，又能同時保有對創作面向的理解與尊重，守護文化流動過程中的開放性，褪去某些自主性追求過程中所裂分的制式框架，這將是未來不分族群、各部落努力進行傳統文化復振時，下一波著作權與傳統智慧創作相關法律朝向愈加成熟的起點。

• 本文作者為紀錄片《日曜日式散步者》導演

聖戰之後

熊儒賢

我非常感激黃秀蘭律師，將這場一九九六年的奧運宣傳主題曲〈歡樂飲酒歌〉席捲全球版權訴訟的硬仗過程，鉅細靡遺的以傳記的方式書寫出來，這個事件不只是為著作權而爭，而是為音樂源起的文化起義，其中唯一可以憑證全貌的當事人就是黃秀蘭。

身為一名在華語樂壇的資深工作者，從主流唱片集團到獨立音樂品牌，其中讓我轉身遠離巨大市場利益的主因就是台灣原住民族的歌聲；當時召喚著已立足在超級主流商業體系的我，好像終於從一個虛擬實境的舞台裡面回到人間。第一次聽到阿美族——郭英男、郭秀珠及馬蘭吟唱隊的老人唱歌，身體跟著歌謠而踏步頓足，完全不用配上任何樂器來烘托編曲，因為深植於部落的數百年傳唱，族人已經可以在吟唱中編出曲式，以獨特「複音」疊唱的層次登上不同的聲音海拔，領唱與答唱彼此呼喚，尤其是在所謂「虛詞」這個歌詞形式的傳達，並不立於世界上任何文字系統，這就是少數民族獨一無二的文化，它的神聖超越文明。

我稱呼郭英男、郭秀珠為「阿公」、「阿嬤」，在音樂上，他們帶我見識了世界之音，在情感上，我是他們沒有血緣的親人。一九九九年十月，我陪著郭英男夫婦及「馬蘭吟唱隊」的老人家們，來到東京參加「愛與夢世界音樂節」，才抵達演出的「澀谷文化會館」，主辦單位協商有一位知名演奏家想要與我們即興合作，基於沒有事前的演出排練，我委婉拒絕了，沒想到郭英男阿公卻答應了願意用〈歡樂飲酒歌〉來做音樂的實驗。「馬蘭吟唱隊」演出十分精采，完整地呈現了「阿美族」的歌謠，觀眾時而亢奮，時而沉靜，直到節目最後主持人邀請即興演奏家與「馬蘭吟唱隊」上台，合作臨場加演的安可曲〈歡樂飲酒歌〉，在後台的我們，開始緊張不安。

我站在側台的台口暗處聆聽、張望，一陣聽不懂的憂傷與演奏協調性不佳的沮喪襲來。曲畢，觀眾拍手甚至起立鼓掌叫好，我墜入了一種不捨的心境，這首歌走掉了原來最美的顏色。

阿公和阿嬤離場時，郭英男第一位下台，嘴裡嘟嚷了一句阿美族的話。

我問郭英男的兒子，阿公剛剛說什麼？

他說：「阿公說，這首歌這樣唱，是一隻雞跟一隻鴨的問題！」

我不太懂阿公這種豁達的感慨。接著回旅館吃飯、睡覺，他們不再談這件事。

而這個一隻雞跟一隻鴨的問題，讓我想了好多年「為什麼」？

從一九九六年郭英男從電視上聽見自己的歌聲出現在奧運宣傳曲之後，他面對的不只是聲音著作被利用的侵權，更是他尊禮於樂的歌唱文化精神，被無知者踐踏與販售，而這個正義與公道，是由滾石唱片和其子品牌魔岩唱片與黃秀蘭律師一路堅持在法律上征戰強權與傲慢才獲得的尊重。我永遠記得一九九九年十二月，當阿公知道〈歡樂飲酒歌〉版權爭議的訴訟達成庭外和解的記者會上，他和妻子郭秀珠雙眼含淚，雙手相挽的互擁畫面。

二〇〇二年三月二十九日我接到郭英男阿公過世的消息之後，當下我決定要用歌聲陪他好好地走。四月十二日在台東阿美族的祖居地（現海濱公園）辦一場「失去單音的和絃」音樂會，請台灣各族群的音樂人出席，每一位認識或不認識郭英男阿公的歌手，義不容辭地答應參加演出。音樂會的隔日是郭英男的出殯儀式，我們跟阿公說再見。中午，我搭火車回台北，在昏昏睡睡中，我猛然驚醒——還記得我提到在日本我不懂為什麼郭英男要答應那個日本即興音樂家的實驗性演出嗎？我突然明白了，阿公是認為我願意唱給全世界聽，我願意用你想要的方式，唱給你聽。郭英男百無禁忌，自由與自然是沒有律法的，他的人是如此，他的歌也是。原住民族的傳統歌謠，最初與最終都會回到跟人跟大自然的關係！

文明的演進需要文化的力量推進，卻不能侵犯原創者的權益，這場官司引發了全球矚目，若不是透過黃秀蘭律師的敘實撰寫，我們永遠不知其原委，也不會知道這首〈歡樂飲酒歌〉來自台灣阿美族的馬蘭部落，由族人郭英男先生所吟唱。

自這場聖戰之後，台灣原住民族年輕人，展開音樂覺醒運動，以吟唱母語歌為榮，傳承了部落文化，復興民謠創作，這起事件也影響了全世界流行音樂界對少數民族音樂的尊重，省思商業體系應對文化歌謠權益的理解，以平等合理的授權方式重建融合式音樂的知法與慎重。

註釋：「馬蘭吟唱隊」由郭英男、郭秀珠、郭秀英、郭國治、郭林姑、陽順英六位阿美族馬蘭部落人士所組成之歌唱團體，平日以務農維生。

● 本文作者為野火樂集 Wild Fire Music, Taiwan 總監

自序

永不流逝的旋律〈歡樂飲酒歌〉

〈歡樂飲酒歌〉國際侵權案，二十餘年前的往事，如今回顧訴訟過程，仍覺歷歷在目。

一九九六年奧林匹克運動會宣傳曲歌聲悠揚傳遍全球之際，一場東、西方的文化侵略征戰，原住民與現代唱片公司的對峙，阿美族音樂與西洋樂曲的抗爭於焉展開；致使奧運蒙塵、音樂變調，最終進入法庭，纏訟多年，公平正義才得以伸張！

〈歡樂飲酒歌〉在台東阿美族群傳唱已久，但走出部落罕為人知。迄至一九九六年美國亞特蘭大奧運開幕，登上世界體育賽事的最高殿堂，世人才得以聆聽它高亢、莊嚴、昂揚的樂曲，但仍無從知悉源自台灣台東的山谷之間。

當一九九六年夏天，阿美族原住民郭英男聽聞自己演唱的歌曲被德國謎樂團（Enigma）盜用，復遭奧運會採為宣傳曲，憂喜交加，喜的是部落的傳世歌曲讓全世界聽見；憂的是為何權益不受尊重？面對西方侵權者鄙夷的態度、貪婪的作風、傲慢的欺凌，在資源稀缺的困境下，郭英男原本不敢奢望討回公道；幸而在滾石／魔岩唱片的力挺下，決心放手一搏，爭取權益。

從來未曾打過官司的郭英男夫婦，為了〈歡樂飲酒歌〉向美國加州聯邦法院提告，經過三年的煎熬，在承審法官嚴屬督促下，兩造歷經漫長談判，終於達成和解。在國內甚至催生了「原住民族傳統智慧創作保護條例」，增訂著作權法保障表演著作的立法例。郭英男〈歡樂飲酒歌〉跨國侵權案也成為智慧財產權法律課程指標案例，傳誦在各大法律學院與音樂產業。

然而，真正侵權行為地的歐洲和美國，卻因資訊缺乏，而對於此案一知半解，甚或以訛傳訛，造成嚴重誤導！數年來世界各國傳聞紛沓，事件真相逐漸消褪。身為侵權訴訟案的主導律師，釐清案件始末責無旁貸；尤其需要以共通語言解說案情經過，因此時隔二十二年後，以中／英文梳理案件，還原事實，交代侵權責任，以正視聽；並呼籲世人共同尊重原住民歌曲與文化，祈願透過美好的音樂，帶給世界真正的和諧與歡樂。

渾厚高亢的歌聲迴盪在山野之間，流轉於奧運舞台，歌曲背後卻藏著貪婪與不尊重。台灣原住民不得已，只好選擇訴諸法律對抗美國唱片公司，多年的國際訴訟，最終在阿美族愛好和平的天性中達成和解，結束法庭審判的殺伐爭戰，讓音樂重回美好的境地。

一 奧運報導出現台灣原住民歌聲

當山海間自然迴盪的原住民歌聲，響徹台東縱谷之際，演唱歌曲的這一對老夫婦怎麼想得到，這首阿美族流傳百年的〈歡樂飲酒歌〉竟然傳唱到奧林匹亞運動會上，甚至引發長達三年的國際音樂著作權訴訟！

接到滾石唱片集團的子公司——魔岩唱片的張培仁總經理Landy來電，我已經在中視晚間新聞播報前的「一九九六亞特蘭大奧運特別報導」看了三天宣傳影片，也聆聽了多次這首奧運宣傳曲。當時只覺得歌聲渾厚高亢，洋溢奧運和平、競爭、寬容、光亮的精神，卻從未想到這樣的樂聲居然來自台灣的阿美族歌唱。

總經理Landy以一貫不疾不徐，低沉富磁性的聲音告知這個驚人的重大事件。語氣中透著隱隱的焦慮，給人些許壓力，他說：「律師，妳還記得上個月我們公司簽的原住民藝人郭英男夫婦嗎？出事了⋯⋯」

怎麼可能忘記呢！這是魔岩唱片簽過的歌手唱片約年紀最大的人，簽約時已經七十三歲，滾石集團內部審慎評估合約的風險及投資的可行性，不過最終在總經理 Landy 推動「原浪潮」──原住民音樂的堅持之下，滾石老板決心將音樂夢想置於商業考量之上，毅然支持總經理的提案。於是滾石唱片排除萬難，以行動和真摯的態度感動部落與家人，終於獲得這位被譽為阿美族最善於歌唱的原住民長老首肯，夫妻倆簽下生平第一份唱片歌手合約。

咦！不是剛簽約嗎？怎麼會出事了？莫非合約出了問題，不會吧！

前幾個月我跟公司法務討論多次，琢磨許久合約才定稿的，怎麼可能一執行就有事？！律師通常心臟要很強，隨時準備迎接無奇不有的悲慘爭端，雖然擬訂修改合約，不會像處理訴訟案件一般刀光劍影，勝負立判。但合約一執行，就看得出律師的功力，倘使合約條文邏輯不通，規範不夠明確，一定會反映在實際操作上，衍生更大的糾紛，所以合約簽署後，在執行過程中，才會測出合約擬訂的優劣。難不成合約沒訂好才出事？我開始忐忑……

郭英男歌聲成為奧運宣傳曲

原來跟那一份歌手合約無關，總經理說出更令人不敢置信的消息：「這幾天中視的奧運特別報導，律師有看嗎？背景音樂好像就是郭英男唱的歌，我們正設法再蒐集更多資料比對聲音。」

「有啊！這幾天晚上我都看奧運特別報導，沈春華當主播嘛，你是說奧運選手的影片配的歌聲嗎？那是阿美族音樂嗎？聽不太出來，只覺得歌聲高亢、渾厚，震懾人心，咦！你怎麼知道呢？是藝人或部落傳來的消息嗎？」我一邊回想昨晚七點多的中視新聞報導片頭的影片，一面覺得奇怪，奧運宣傳曲怎麼會用到我們台灣原住民的歌聲？

「剛才郭英男他們在台東打電話過來說的，前兩天部落族人聽收音機，聽到奧運的報導，立刻發現背景音樂是郭英男的聲音，趕快告訴郭英男。

他們家人一起看中視新聞確認是他唱的，感到很疑惑又生氣，為什麼奧運用他的歌卻沒告訴他？他們就去找台東一位議員請教要怎麼處理，了解事情梗概後，議員跟他們說這種事情跟法律有關，要找律師處理，民意代表幫不上忙，因為可能涉及侵權訴訟。郭老先生也沒認識什麼律師，後來想到有跟唱片公司簽約，就問公司怎麼辦，剛剛製作部同仁才告訴我發生這等大事，我向三毛（滾石老闆段鍾潭）報告後，三毛叫我立刻諮詢律師，這是不是一個音樂侵權事件？我們要怎麼處理？」Landy 清楚交代消息來源與事件背景。

歌聲比對鑑定

「奧運歌曲到底有沒有侵權，還是要先確認是不是郭英男的歌聲。你們手上有奧運的宣傳影片跟郭英男的錄音帶或 CD 嗎？必須先用精密的音響設備同步比對，確定是他的歌聲後，才能判定是否構成侵權。」我先提醒侵權的前提事實及證據的鑑定問題，繼之一想又問道：「奇怪，公司不是還沒幫郭英男錄製唱片嗎？奧運是用哪首歌曲，怎麼拿到郭英男的錄音帶，是他以前還沒簽約時唱的嗎？」

「目前無從得知是怎麼拿到郭英男的音樂，郭家的人說奧運用的是〈歡樂飲酒歌〉。這首歌他們在豐年祭都會唱，是有人錄下來，或是什麼時候請郭英男夫婦唱的，現在還不清楚。事情剛發生，資訊還太少，不過我已經請同事側錄中視的奧運報導背景音樂，還有拜託郭英男的家人從台東寄他以前唱的這首歌錄音帶來比對，應該下午會送到，律師傍晚有空嗎？請妳來公司一起聽，辨認一下，我們再討論怎麼處理這個緊急狀況。」Landy 危機處理經驗豐富，立刻付諸行動。

「好，我四點過去公司討論。」我掛斷電話，趕緊交代法務助理盡量蒐集奧運宣傳影片的資訊，我開始找著作權法關於音樂著作及錄音著作的相關規定，再查原住民的音樂有沒有特別規定，後來想到今年奧運在美國亞特蘭大舉行，侵權行為地在美國，於是接著查詢美國著作權法的規定。

同時研究如果確定屬於侵權事件，究竟侵害什麼人、什麼權利？不過，還沒能建立整個事件的思考架構，就趕著要到魔岩唱片公司開會了。

踏進魔岩總經理辦公室，看到 Landy 戴著專業耳機，面對辦公桌後面的大型音響專注地聆聽，轉身看到我，立刻拔掉耳機的插頭，放音樂給我聽，一面解釋：「這是郭英男的歌聲，出現在『謎』樂團（Enigma）《徘徊不定》（The Cross of Changes）專輯中〈返璞歸真〉（Return to innocence）這首曲子中，律師妳聽聽看。」

音樂流瀉一地，先是前奏，接上原住民歌聲〈歡樂飲酒歌〉，穿插英文唱腔，搭配得天衣無縫，自然順暢，歌曲長度四分十五秒。聽畢一曲，Landy 接著放奧運宣傳曲，音樂完全相同，但是樂曲較短，最後將這兩首歌曲分由兩部音響同步播放，完全重疊，無法區分，Landy 以他專業的音樂鑑賞力斷定是同一首歌。

侵權成立嗎？

關掉音響後，Landy 問了郭英男夫婦心中最深的疑問：「亞特蘭大奧運會侵權了嗎？」

我下結論。

「使用原住民的音樂與歌聲，沒經過原住民的同意，就成立侵權。」

Landy 帶著我走到另一棟大樓——滾石唱片公司的辦公室，進了總經理室，Landy 報告方才鑑定歌曲的意見及我的看法後，滾石老闆段鍾潭只提出一個問題：「奧運歌曲有侵權嗎？」

我點點頭，三毛說了一句話揭開了這樁聞名世界的國際音樂侵權訴訟的序幕：「那麼我們就開始吧！進入法律程序。」

三毛問我多少時間可以整理初步的法律意見及採取步驟，我說大約四個小時。三毛轉頭指示 Landy：「我們今天晚上十點開會，請製作部、企宣部及負責郭英男藝人的部門經理全部與會，由律師先分析法律觀點及建議，我們討論處理策略及執行方式。」Landy 頻頻點頭後，疾步走向辦公室分頭交代祕書聯繫，我立刻回到事務所準備法律意見書。

這是個難熬的下午，由於侵權事實涉及多國的樂團、音樂製作公司、唱片發行商，我必須在晚上開會前的短短四個小時內，研究這個跨越三十年（一九六六年至一九九六年）、橫渡三大洲（亞洲、歐洲、美洲）原住民歌曲的案情。事實面的資訊極少，法律規定卻須適用多達五個國家地區──台灣、美國、法國、英國、德國的著作權法，僅僅是台灣的著作權法從民國五十五年到現在八十五年，立法院就修改了六次，我快速地查詢台灣著作權的歷史沿革，確認各階段的著作權法都有保護詞曲、錄音，而且保護年限都涵蓋在歌曲各階段中。一陣緊湊的查閱分析中，突然安心了下來，因為這首歌確實有受到法律的保護，如此一來採取法律途徑就師出有名了。

二 〈歡樂飲酒歌〉著作權保護分析

可是接下來的問題更頭痛了，這首〈歡樂飲酒歌〉可以被保護的到底是什麼「著作」呢？是詞曲音樂著作，或是歌聲——表演著作、錄音著作？

這首歌似乎不是郭英男作曲填詞，而是部落長老傳唱的老歌，錄音帶也不是他錄製的，所以「詞曲音樂著作權」及「歌曲錄音著作權」絕對不是他可以主張的，那麼「編曲」、「演唱」呢？聽說郭英男曾改編此首歌曲的旋律，而且可以確定的是，奧委會使用的歌曲是郭英男夫婦演唱的歌聲，剛剛在 Landy 的辦公室比對過的，毫無疑義，只是我國的著作權法有保護「表演著作」嗎？

我立刻翻閱一九六六及一九七八年的中華民國著作權法，其中完全沒提到「表演著作」。心頭一驚！是不是演唱歌曲不在著作權法保護之列？

查了半個多小時才發現當年立法過程中，立法委員認為「表演著作」可以涵蓋在「舞蹈戲劇」中，毋庸另外明文規定，就省略「表演著作」這個項目了。可是「歌唱表演」可以列入「舞蹈戲劇」中嗎？這些立委哀哀諸公怎麼沒有考慮到這一點呢？眼下迫於時間緊急，也只好認同立委的講法，根據「舞蹈戲劇」的著作權規定主張演唱者郭英男有「表演著作權」了，至於「編曲」的音樂著作權恐怕要再向郭英男本人查證，才能有定論。

匆匆地將這些法律規定，包括魔岩唱片提供的有限資訊，以及幾個小時研究的心得整理重點，八點多回到家，隨意吃了幾口飯，拿了資料就衝到會議場所。那是滾石唱片老闆三毛家附近的餐廳，晚上十點不到，滾石一級主管與魔岩唱片總經理 Landy 都到了，一會兒三毛也出現了，面對這種跨國侵權案，大家都嚴陣以待。

三毛一坐定，第一句話就問：「Is this a case?」這件案子成立嗎？

我篤定地點點頭，三毛說：「好！我們開始討論。」Landy 先說明這個侵權事件的爆發緣由，以及這幾天案情的發展、郭英男的態度與部落的反應，我接下來解釋侵權事實的重點與法律上可以主張的權利。分析法律的立場過程中，與會的主管紛紛拋出各種疑點，同時提議採取的因應策略，包括召開記者會、提出侵權訴訟、籲請政府機關出面協助、要求奧運及時停止使用侵權歌曲……各式各樣的意見一一出籠，三毛都靜靜地聆聽，讓大家暢所欲言，腦力激盪。到了凌晨一點，三毛表示必須離席回家照顧小孩，離開前說明妳的法律上見解，好嗎？」

三毛問我：「律師，妳的看法呢？妳建議我們怎麼做？

深夜危機處理會議

我說：「我提議先確定郭英男的立場，如果他決定要委任唱片公司處理全案，請他先簽署授權書，因為這個案子明天一曝光，媒體報導後必然會受到各方矚目，很多雜音會出現，部落也會介入，眼前首要亟務是先穩定當事人的心情，確定書面的授權，唱片公司才有資格處理這個跨國侵權案。」三毛立刻指示 Landy 明天聯繫郭英男，簽署侵權案委任授權書。

我繼續分析：「此案有幾個重大疑點還未釐清，我認為應該先查證清楚，包括當年郭英男演唱〈歡樂飲酒歌〉的錄音狀況，錄音如何授權？他一九八八年到法國表演究竟詳情為何？必須先向關鍵人士或政府機關查證，關鍵點查清楚再召開記者會，才不會發布錯誤訊息。」

Landy 立即附議，交代祕書聯絡安排明天拜訪此案關鍵人士，至於政府機關的查詢就由我正式發函處理。

臨走前我再強調：「接下來最重要的是，如何面對目前持續播放此首歌曲的奧委會，我建議以最快的速度委聘美國律師發函警告，要求奧委會立刻停播這首〈歡樂飲酒歌〉，並且向原唱者郭英男夫婦公開致歉，賠償侵權損失。倘使奧委會誠意十足，願意跟我們和解，最佳的和解方案就是在七月十九日奧運閉幕式邀請郭英男到亞特蘭大奧運現場演唱這首歌，讓全世界看到。」

此時大家聽了都熱血沸騰，整間餐廳氣氛高亢喧譁到極點，只有三毛依舊冷靜清醒地確認策略方向與分配工作項目。我在凌晨兩點離開後，聽說他們繼續討論到凌晨四點，確定危機處理的分工架構及排序。

〈歡樂飲酒歌〉演唱錄製大事紀

翌日，我一進辦公室，把昨晚會議中唱片公司主管提供的資料，逐一整理分析，按照年份、事件、單位區分歸類，初步拼湊出大致的事件輪廓：

1. 〈歡樂飲酒歌〉在阿美族稱為〈第二首長歌〉，每年豐年祭中常被演唱，郭英男為部落中公認歌唱者之翹楚，多年來擔任重祭典活動之領唱者。

2. 民俗音樂學者Ｘ教授曾在西元一九六六進行民俗樂曲田野採集過程中，於一九七八年到台東尋訪郭英男夫婦錄製他們演唱〈歡樂飲酒歌〉。

3.郭英男夫婦於一九七九年曾受 X 教授之邀，前往台北第一唱片公司錄音室錄製〈歡樂飲酒歌〉並且發行唱片《台灣有聲資料庫全集〈傳統民歌篇〉1》。

4.在一九八八年文建會的安排下，由 X 教授擔任理事長之 X 藝術基金會邀集多個部落知名原住民演唱者與團體參加太平洋藝術節活動，郭英男夫婦及馬蘭吟唱隊也在受邀之列，組團飛往歐洲各國去表演原住民音樂舞蹈。

5.在一九八八年法國巴黎的法國文化之家表演時，郭英男曾上台演唱〈歡樂飲酒歌〉，法國文化之家作成現場錄音，事後要集結當天演唱之原住民歌曲製作專輯 CD，但發現〈歡樂飲酒歌〉的錄音品質不佳，法國文化之家向 X 教授索取錄音帶，X 教授提供錄音帶，但究竟錄音帶是一九七八年田野採集的錄音或一九七九年第一唱片的錄音尚待查證，法國文化之家製成 CD 並支付相當於三千元法郎的授權金予 X 藝術基金

6. 德國瑪寶唱片公司（Mambo）聘請謎樂團委託製作人克里圖（Michael Cretu）製作《徘徊不定》專輯唱片，克里圖在德國一家小唱片行發現法國文化之家發行的台灣原住民複音歌唱 CD，選取其中一首〈歡樂飲酒歌〉，改編混音為歌曲〈返璞歸真〉，由英國維京唱片公司（Virgin）透過 EMI 唱片公司於一九九三年在全球發行專輯唱片。

7. 奧委會於一九九六年經由 EMI 唱片公司授權，將改編的〈歡樂飲酒歌〉即〈返璞歸真〉作為亞特蘭大奧運宣傳曲，授權全球各國播映奧運宣傳影片時使用。

　　事件發展的梗概大致理出頭緒了，可是很多人、事、時、地、物的細節無法確認。尤其是關鍵的歌曲授權經過無從得悉，我與滾石、魔岩唱片公司決定親自登門拜訪關鍵人士——X 教授，一窺當年故事發展的究竟，才能進一步評估法律程序如何進行、提告與否。能不能啟動一場跨國的侵權訴訟，由原住民出面控訴國際唱片公司侵害著作權，端視後續案情的揭露與發現了。

在滾石老闆緊急召開會議，我決定承接〈歡樂飲酒歌〉侵權案之後，各組人馬在三毛分工指派工作下，積極推動，分進合擊。魔岩唱片總經理Landy發揮最高的效率，透過滾石集團綿密的人際網絡，在不到十二小時內已聯繫上這樁侵權案的關鍵人士——X教授。當時X教授擁有國策顧問、X藝術基金會理事長頭銜，我們完全沒有把握他會答應與我們見面，尤其在擬將提告的敏感時節前夕，這位台灣的音樂界重量級人士，願意告訴我們多少事實真相？特別是跟他個人有關的歌曲授權部分，究竟實情為何？享有高知名度、崇高地位的他可能吐實嗎？

拜訪關鍵人士──民俗音樂學者

帶著忐忑不安的心情，Landy 拎著伴手禮，我們相約在公車站附近的公園，兩人走入巷弄尋訪 X 教授的住處，繞了好幾條巷道終於找到了。按門鈴之前，我們已演練過提問的重要問題，包括當年田野採集的歌曲、領軍參加歐洲藝術節的過程，返國後提供〈歡樂飲酒歌〉的轉折，以及這些故事過程中有無完成授權手續。我們約好原則上由 Landy 發言，我只需適時補充或提問，以免律師開口，主導訪談，引發學者的不悅與壓力。

踏入 X 教授家門後，Landy 不負所託，以他一貫穩定中帶有磁性的聲音，先敘說來訪緣由，接著禮貌性地請教 X 教授當年的往事。X 教授平和地坐在典雅的椅上，溫文有禮地回顧三十年前著手的民俗音樂田野採集歷程，提到了他親自到台東造訪郭英男夫婦欣賞演唱的情節，又敘說極力促成各原住民族組團前往瑞士、巴黎、歐洲、各大城市的光榮事蹟，眼睛閃爍著欣慰與愉快的光芒。聽著溫煦的長者將陳年美事娓娓道來，我們都沉醉在歷史的榮耀歡樂中。

眼看夜愈來愈深，X教授的夫人催促吃藥就寢，我擔心此行主要任務未達，向Landy示意，提醒他趕緊詢問在台東錄音或巴黎表演錄音有無授權的事。Landy似乎一時沒意會過來，繼續聆聽，未發一語，於是我只好鼓起勇氣問了這個尖銳的問題。原本含笑盈盈處處流露學者風範的X教授聞之臉色不變，開始訓斥晚輩：「你們這麼年輕，完全無法想像在民國七十幾年台灣國際地位的艱難，我們在中華民國退出聯合國，與世界很多重要國家斷交後，可以爭取到帶著台灣原住民前往歐洲各國重要城市表演，極其不易！這是外交上異常艱鉅的任務，這些原住民的演唱舞蹈表演處處獲得熱烈的歡迎，在那個時代，這是多麼不容易的外交成果，妳卻追問我有沒有授權？有沒有簽約？巴黎法國文化之家樂意將我們來自台灣的原住民表演錄音下來，這是多麼光榮的事，還需要什麼授權簽約?!妳曉不曉得歐洲國家著作權觀念濃厚，怎麼可能侵權？你們追查此事應該到此為止。」

表明當年組團突破外交困境的心跡之後，X教授繼續說：「後來法國文化之家的館長說要把這些原住民的音樂製作CD，放在他們館裡保存，我也覺得很好呀，推廣我們台灣原住民音樂嘛！後來館長告訴我當天他們現場錄音效果不好，問我有沒有其他的錄音帶？我就把以前在第一唱片發行的專輯錄音帶裡面，郭英男有唱到〈歡樂飲酒歌〉的帶子寄給他，之後聽說外國的唱片公司用到這首歌發專輯，我寫信問法國文化之家，他們也馬上寄了版稅來，我就代表基金會同意，都有經過正式簽約授權嘛！」

三 表演者郭英男夫婦有無授權？

問題是演唱者郭英男夫婦有沒有授權？這是重點呀！如果源頭沒授權，縱使歌曲的錄製單位——法國文化之家或藝術基金會完成授權手續，還是不合法啊！望著微慍的學者，我很猶豫要不要再提出另外一題絕對會觸怒他的疑問，看到 Landy 急忙打圓場安撫 X 教授的情緒後，我決定依然要提問，因為在今夜拜訪之後，全案進入法律程序，很可能再無探知真相的機會了。

果然律師提問都會觸及當事人最敏感的神經，我一詢問：「在第一唱片的錄音及法國文化之家館方的錄音，請問郭英男有同意嗎？」

X 教授凌厲眼神射向我，不悅地說：「都是往事了，他們都唱了，有什麼同意不同意呢？」

我決定再斗膽加碼問一句：「那麼後來法國文化之家館長請您提供〈歡樂飲酒歌〉的錄音帶，X教授有經過郭英男夫婦的同意嗎？」

X教授索性站起來表示送客，我定定地看著他，如如不動，等待答案。

他走到玄關打開大門，說道：「錄音帶是X藝術基金會的，為什麼需要他們的同意?!」此際Landy與我只好識趣地起身走到門邊，禮貌地告別。

我們走出X教授的家，心中仍有很多疑問與不以為然。那一年我與Landy才三十幾歲，年輕氣盛，追問事實未果，帶著滿腹問號，我們信步走到附近的公園，Landy提問下一步怎麼做？「看起來整個歷程就是沒得到演唱者的授權，還講得義正辭嚴，什麼突破外交困境、民族的榮耀……律師，現在怎麼辦？」

「我覺得也不太能責怪X教授的心態，當年台灣的國際地位與處境確實非常艱難，能帶領原住民走出去，登上國際舞台誠屬不易！況且當時台灣社會各階層著作權法的意識也很薄弱，他的想法恐怕也是一般人普遍的觀點，而且在那個時代，學者或有社經地位的人常會為了追求某種榮耀或光環，提出冠冕堂皇的口號，合理化他們的的作為，而忽略個人權益。再說整個案件中，我們恐怕不適宜與他為敵，他的身分、地位都很關鍵，我們得善用這顆棋子，最好能促使他站在郭英男這邊，共同討伐外國的侵權。」

我凝視著公園昏黃的街燈與天際的滿月，提出心中的感想，Landy 點點頭，無奈地接受，我們分頭回家。

回到家裡，我再度抱著各國著作權法資料，繼續加班，研究侵權的主體及違反的各年代法律規定，確認後要整理交給魔岩唱片，協助郭英男夫婦委託美國加州洛杉磯的律師事務所 Dwewey Ballantine 撰擬律師函。美國律師事務所作業的同時，在國內我們仍持續查證當年事件發生的疑點，試圖藉由不同管道詢問相關人士，將整個事件拼湊完整的輪廓。

遲來的授權金可以收下嗎？

我除了尋訪郭英男的親友回溯一九七八年錄音的狀況外，進一步寄發信函予文建會及 X 藝術基金會，請他們提供一九八八年郭英男夫婦赴法國表演的經過及曾簽署的文件。八十五年七月五日我寄出律師函，X 藝術基金會回信表示，當年他們並非主辦單位，故未保存任何相關文件；倒是關於謎樂團製作《徘徊不定》專輯唱片時，曾取得法國文化之家分配一半的授權金，在 X 藝術基金會的聲明下，法國文化之家分配一半的授權金予 X 藝術基金會，基金會願意將這筆款項與郭英男夫婦均分。

五千元法郎予 X 藝術基金會，我期期以為不可，郭英男請家人詢問我和唱片公司可否收下這筆錢，我建議郭英男家屬思考，他們是否收了一萬五千元法郎或其中一半，就可接受目前全盤事件的發展？思索數日之後，那麼就沒有資格提告侵權了。我建議郭英男家屬思考，他們是否收了一萬五千元法郎或其中一半，就可接受目前全盤事件的發展？思索數日之後，此案即將進入法律程序，在這個節骨眼收取版稅，不啻事後追認授權，他們也覺得不合理，世人終究不了解真相，也不知道〈歡樂飲酒歌〉來自台灣，郭英男家人認為事情不應該以此種方式結束，於是決定拒收這筆遲來的授權金。

還原當年實況

二十天後文建會回覆，僅表示會內並無郭氏夫婦赴法國表演的相關文件資料。文建會的回覆如此簡略，令人意外，如果依照 X 教授的講法，在當年國際情勢艱困下，文建會得以受邀帶領原住民團體赴歐表演，是何等的大事，為什麼官方遍尋書面文件紀錄不著？本於律師研究案情蒐集證據的精神，我不死心地繼續尋求相關的線索，終於找到一九八八年陪同出國的重要人士之一──徐韶仁口述部分事實。透過電話他回憶往事，說道：

「文建會委託徐瀛洲組團出國表演曾經簽約，但合約已經遺失，文建會也曾與法國文化之家簽約。當時郭英男等原住民上台表演，法國文化之家在現場欲進行錄音時，徐瀛洲曾出面當場提出異議，而文建會並無任何人員出面交涉或阻止；至於 X 教授是否允諾法國文化之家作成現場表演的錄音，並無所悉。」

到底這席話是否符合真實狀況，我與魔岩唱片都沒有把握，於是我們決定再深入追查，三天後循線尋訪一九八八年任職文建會第三處表演藝術科擔任視察的黃武忠，曾隨團出國，擔任財務及行政工作。黃武忠表示文建會當年未曾與法國文化之家簽約，但雙方傳真文件往來有包含「同意書」，文建會確實曾與帶團的徐瀛洲簽訂委託契約，可是郭英男上台表演時，對於法國文化之家依慣例錄音的動作，文建會現場人員由於不諳法文，無人出面交涉。

顯然這些官員也無法提供當年的文件，那麼究竟文建會有無書面同意法國文化之家同意現場表演錄音，已成羅生門，無法證實。縱使有書面同意，如果沒有獲得表演者本人的同意，也無法發生法律效力，追根究柢，繞了一大圈還是要回頭向郭英男夫婦確認，從一九六六年 X 教授開始進行原住民音樂田野採集至一九七八年在台東錄音，及一九七九年前往台北第一唱片錄音室，一直到一九八八年法國表演現場錄音有無同意，或者收受酬金？

郭英男雖然已屆七十四歲的高齡，記憶力倒是一點不輸年輕人，往事歷歷，娓娓道來，他說：「民國六十七年 X 教授來台東叫我們唱歌，說要錄音，那時候是用一台很簡單的錄音機在錄，……他沒有給我們什麼啊！只有帶一瓶小米酒來送我們。第二年到台北錄音，也沒有什麼表示呀。那次到法國表演，我也不知道有錄音，他們叫我上去表演我就上去了，我太太沒有一起唱，因為她身體不太舒服，坐在下面，外國人講什麼我們都聽不懂，文建會派誰去我也不認識，只有 X 教授我們見過，不過，在法國表演，他也沒跟我們講什麼事。」

看來是可以下結論了，郭英男並沒有同意任何人將他的演唱〈歡樂飲酒歌〉錄音授權給法國文化之家或 EMI 唱片改編或製作專輯發行，因此不論是法國文化之家、EMI 唱片公司或亞特蘭大奧運使用〈歡樂飲酒歌〉的演唱錄音都涉及侵權。

侵權過程之事實整理

在查證事實及侵權情節的同時，我也針對跨時三十年（一九六六至一九九六年）的相關國家著作權法分析研究完畢，整理出郭英男對於〈歡樂飲酒歌〉擁有的權利，至少包含歌曲旋律的改編權（編曲之音樂著作權）及演唱的表演著作權。於是我整理了這個侵權案的事實：

1. 台灣台東阿美族（Amis）經過世代創作、傳承、發展出〈第二首長歌〉（母語「巴拉芳」即「歡樂飲酒歌」），經郭英男先生重新編曲，與其妻郭秀珠女士以對位與合聲之形式演唱。於民國六十七年，音樂學者 X

教授進行台灣全省民俗音樂田野調查工作，錄製了由郭英男夫婦演唱之〈歡樂飲酒歌〉。整個錄音是在台東郭英男先生親戚家中完成的，此外，尚錄製其他首歌曲。在錄音當時，郭英男夫婦口頭同意並允許 X 教授於教學目的下使用此錄音著作。然而，X 教授卻在未為郭英男夫婦知悉之情形下，逕將上述〈歡樂飲酒歌〉之錄音製作成卡帶販售，稍後並發行 CD 版本，而將此錄音著作存放於 X 藝術基金會（Chinese Folk Art Foundation 簡稱 CFAF）。

2. 民國七十七年五月法國文化教育部（French Ministry of Culture and Education）邀請 X 藝術基金會帶領台灣原住民前往巴黎世界文化會館參加「太平洋地區原住民舞蹈音樂節」。在行政院文化建設委員會之資助下，郭英男夫婦隨同 X 藝術基金會赴法演出。在世界文化會館演出過程中，法國文化之家（Maison Des Cultures Du Monde 簡稱 MDCDM）未徵得郭英男等人之同意，錄下其現場演唱之歌聲，其後欲與尚收錄部分 X 藝術基金會於民國六十七年蒐集之民俗音樂，製作為「台灣原住民複音歌唱」（Polyphonies Vocales Des Aborigenes De Taiwan）鐳射唱片發行。但由於在世界文化會館之錄音品質未盡理想，法國文化之家乃向 X 教授要求提供錄音效果較好的〈歡樂飲酒歌〉，X 教授隨即提供在民國六十八年第一唱片錄製發行的〈歡樂飲酒歌〉予法國文化之家，其間並無任何讓渡文件。鐳射唱片之發行封面標寫法國文化之家與 X 藝術基金會，但未註明演唱者郭英男夫婦之姓名。

3. 民國八十二年德國維京唱片公司（Virgin Record Company of Germany）委託瑪寶音樂公司（Mambo Musik Company）為謎樂團製作《徘徊不定》唱片專輯。於同年四月四日，瑪寶音樂公司交付一筆款項予法國文化之家。四月十九日，瑪寶公司製作人克里圖與法國文化之家簽訂合約，取得授權使用〈歡樂飲酒歌〉。之後即將之糅合現代舞曲旋律編入〈返璞歸真〉單曲中。該授權合約明定，法國文化之家保證其享有母帶之所有權且經合法授權；此外，法國文化之家聲明，所有他們及藝人可主張的權利皆已轉讓。《徘徊不定》專輯一經發行，立即躍居告示排行榜全世界前一百名並連續蟬聯三十二週，且持續四週保持全球第四名，銷售量亦超過六百萬張。此專輯在台灣是由台灣科藝百代（EMI）唱片公司代理發行；在美國則是由 Virgin Schallplatten GmbH 獨家授權給克里斯瑪唱片公司（Charisma Records America）紐約的公司發行。該專輯鐳射唱片是由加州 EMI 唱片公司（Capitol-EMI Music）之子公司 Capitol Records, Inc. 製造。

4. 民國八十四年八月 X 藝術基金會理事長寄發一份著作權聲明書（Copyright Statement）予法國文化之家，此聲明書之相關部分，聲明 X 藝術基金會所發行之任何錄音著作，其著作權歸原始演唱者所有，或視為歸原始演唱之民族團體所有，因為他們應被視為該音樂之著作人或作曲者。理事長於民國八十四年八月間與法國文化之家洽商後，法國文化之家匯寄壹萬伍仟法郎予 X 藝術基金會。

5. 民國八十五年美國亞特蘭大夏季奧運會使用〈返璞歸真〉一曲中〈歡樂飲酒歌〉之樂曲片段作為奧運宣傳短片之配樂，使用過程並未標明演唱者為郭英男夫婦或支付任何權利金予郭英男夫婦。

上述侵權案的事實提供給滾石高層後，三毛與 Landy 一讀完，立刻決定正式委託美國律師寄發律師函給 EMI 唱片公司、奧運委員會及法國文化之家，提出侵權賠償的明確訴求，限期回應，否則進入法律訴訟。

〈歡樂飲酒歌〉跨國訴訟開了第一槍，接下來是戰是和，就看這些侵權者如何回應了。

國內反對聲浪四起

阿美族原住民的音樂遭侵權，台灣各界咸感震驚，媒體披露後，各界關心及批評紛至沓來，有人譴責外國唱片公司及奧運，有人為阿美族音樂登上國際舞台而喝采。不過，在探討〈歡樂飲酒歌〉演唱者郭英男夫婦有無權利？可否提告？幾乎國內智慧財產權產、官、學各界都一面倒，傾向於演唱者沒有詞曲音樂著作權，他們普遍認為〈歡樂飲酒歌〉不是郭英男作詞作曲，而是阿美族部落世代傳唱的歌曲；郭英男也沒有表演著作權，因為著作權缺乏相關規定；更沒有專輯錄音著作權，因為不是郭英男錄製的。

唱片公司看了這些排山倒海的負面報導，憂心忡忡，尤其連內政部著作權委員會的官員接受電視台的採訪時都表示，原住民對於這首〈歡樂飲酒歌〉並不享有任何權利時，更是差點澆熄我們這群正在為郭英男夫婦辛苦爭取權益團隊的信心。不過基於多年緊密合作建立的信賴關係，滾石唱片集團對我提出的法律立場完全信任與接納，因此縱使外界一片否定聲中，我們依然積極籌備侵權案的各項布局，在最急迫短促的時間內，我與滾石高層再度開會共商對策，包括法律訴訟、媒體因應、事實蒐證等重要步驟的展開與落實。

會議中推動此案進入法律程序的共識達成後，一組人馬負責尋求聯繫美國大型律師事務所，因為主戰場在美國，第一波法律動作勢必要在美國發生，趕在奧運舉辦期間祭出法律手段，才能收到最大的效果。沒想到我們的提告對象——EMI 唱片及奧委會勢力太過強大，正式詢問的十家美國知名法律事務所，只有兩家願意進一步接觸洽談，其他八家表示不願意得罪 EMI 唱片公司而放棄合作機會。甚至尋找美國媒體公關公司協助時，多數遭到斷然回絕，理由也是不欲與 EMI 唱片公司對立，而唯一有興趣的一家公關公司索價甚高，滾石老闆只好忍痛割捨在美國發動媒體戰的策略，把時間精力專注於美國律師事務所的合作洽談。

召開記者會表明立場

可是國內的媒體報導，我們卻不得不面對。在媒體無孔不入的突兀紛亂狀況下，有些記者直闖台東郭英男家中專訪、有些採訪學者官員放出負面消息、有些向唱片公司打探軍情，連外國媒體也加入搶新聞的戰局，魔岩唱片索性宣布，確定在民國八十五年七月二日召開記者會對外說明。

記者會前夕唱片公司邀請郭英男夫婦來到台北，我帶著事先擬就的中英文委託書請他們夫妻簽署。在飯店休息時，剛巧大家分頭在忙，我與郭英男單獨聊天，他生平第一次與律師講話，神色有些拘謹靦腆，我想著如何讓老人家心情放鬆一些。我們坐在窗邊，望向窗外燈光閃爍的台北市夜景，我隨大家的叫法，開口問道：「阿公，來台北心情如何？覺得台北怎麼樣？」

郭英男看看窗外沉思好一會兒，答說：「台北的房子都好小，好像火柴盒……。」

我隨意提到：「台北房子多、車多、人也多，阿公會不會一到台北，就想回故鄉？」

郭英男果然笑著說：「我現在最想的，還是在我們台東的山谷中唱歌。」難得有這麼一個空檔時刻，提到他喜愛的歌唱，阿公像孩子般開懷地笑了。

當天晚間魔岩公司傳真記者會邀請函與新聞稿的草稿過來，我看過修改定稿後，魔岩企宣人員以最快速度傳送給各家媒體記者，平面和電子媒體無一遺漏。

郭英男記者會招待會

目前 Enigma 的暢銷單曲〈Return to the Innocence〉在全世界已銷售有數百萬張之譜，並且於近期被選為一九九六年奧運主題曲。然而當這首歌被世人廣為傳唱的同時，卻很少人知道在〈Return to the Innocence〉這首歌中出現的空靈歌聲，卻是出於台灣台東的原住民夫婦——郭英男夫婦。

從 Enigma 到奧運會的主題曲，整個過程當中，郭英男夫婦並未受到他們應該享有的公平對待與基本尊重，迄今整個事件已受到全世界媒體高度關注，並且透過國內外各媒體的逐漸披露，世人已開始對這事件稍有了解。

然因牽連甚廣，事件的來龍去脈仍混沌不清。因此郭英男覺得有其必要，召開公開記者會，親自交代事件的始末與個人主張。

郭英男夫婦與其阿美族領唱團等六人，已於一九九六年一月與魔岩唱片簽約。除了授權魔岩為其錄製專輯外，並決定將所有法律相關事務委託魔岩代為處理。記者會當天，魔岩將偕同郭英男夫婦宣布，未來相關法律事務的處理方向與作法。

魔岩企宣部同時發布新聞稿聲明：

聯絡人：魔岩唱片

北市敦化南路二段二〇一號

地點：遠東飯店地下一樓　洛北秀南廳

時間：八十五年七月二日（二）下午二點

魔岩唱片公司自即日起正式協助郭英男先生夫婦處理〈歡樂飲酒歌〉侵權爭議，委託黃秀蘭律師為其法律顧問，並著手進行有關之查證工作。

另外，魔岩唱片公司也在此鄭重表示，如有任何法律事務而產生的金錢收益，魔岩唱片將不會從中獲取任何利益。

魔岩唱片已代郭英男先生夫婦在所有前述相關單位之所在地尋求律師，我們當然非常願意看見郭先生夫婦的歌聲在全世界被傳唱，也很榮幸這首歌能在奧運中流傳，但是在查證後，如確認有任何單位明確地侵犯了郭英男先生的基本權益，就將對其採取法律行動，無論對方是政府、國際公司甚至是奧委會。

我與 Landy 在七月二日早上叮嚀郭英男夫婦在記者會上只需表明以下立場：奧運播放宣傳曲確實是他們夫妻演唱、決定透過法律程序爭取權益，委託律師打國際官司獲得賠償，最重要的是讓全世界知道這首歌來自台東阿美族的聲音。

郭英男聽完點點頭，不過，澄澈的目光有一絲黯然，我問他怎麼了？

阿公說：「我一輩子沒有上過法院，沒想到這麼老了才要打官司……」

我笑一笑說：「阿公！別擔心，您只要出面說明立場，其他的交給我們處理。」他臉色漸趨和緩，沒再多言。

四　魔岩唱片決定展開國際訴訟

當天記者會順利完成，經媒體報導後，各方熱烈迴響，但討論者眾、欲趁機出名者也多。社會各界普遍看法仍認為郭英男並未擁有此首歌曲之權利，預期這場即將發生的國際侵權訴訟可能以敗訴收場，只有著作權事務的主管機關——內政部著作權委員會開始轉變態度，主動協助，並指派科長定期關心此案了解進度，給予官方支持。但也僅止於定期來電關心詢問，或提供相關法規資訊，至於真正面對國際侵權者，所涉及的法律事務及各項折衝談判，還是要靠當事人和唱片公司自行奮鬥爭取，政府機關對於史上第一次國內原住民遭遇音樂著作權遭受外國侵害，依然束手無策，無法站在特定的高度給予法律、人力、行政各方面資源的援助，受害的原住民只好自求多福了。在國內政府機關、學術機構及民間普遍反應侵權案勝算極低的狀態下，滾石集團與魔岩唱片毫不退縮，取得郭英男夫婦堅定的允諾與表示後，決定展開國際訴訟，向侵權者宣示爭取權益的決心。

不過持續兩週多數媒體報導，依然傾向不利於郭英男夫婦爭取權利的立場。魔岩唱片與我咸感不平，萌生孤軍奮戰的感觸，滾石與魔岩唱片高層及企宣人員疲於應付各方媒體車輪戰，正欲研商對策之際，剛巧台北市政府表態聲援，樂意為郭英男夫婦召開記者會力表支持。Landy 向三毛報告市府訊息後，滾石高層決定接受北市府的邀約，七月十八日指派專人帶領郭英男夫婦從台東專程北上，參加翌日在台北市政府召開的國際記者會。

台北市政府公開表態支持

民國八十五年七月十九日中午兩點記者會才會開始，一點鐘我與 Landy 已抵達會場，在外面走廊再度討論並確認記者會流程：先由 Landy 開場說明事件背景，接著介紹郭英男、郭秀珠夫婦及馬蘭吟唱隊，同時請郭英男敘說說心情與決定，Landy 繼續說明整個侵權案疑點與唱片公司立場，再由我宣布即將採取的法律途徑，約莫進行三十至四十分鐘後，開放媒體發問十至十五分鐘，最後請郭英男夫婦與馬蘭吟唱隊在現場演唱〈歡樂飲酒歌〉，在歌聲迴盪中結束記者會。

中午兩點前，遠東飯店地下一樓記者會現場已擠滿記者，攝影機架設整排，攝影記者忙著選定位置取景，文字記者有些翻閱魔岩唱片發放的新聞稿，有些電話聯繫電視台晚上播映新聞的時間。會場同時播放郭英男夫婦的〈歡樂飲酒歌〉，氣氛愈來愈熱烈喧鬧，直到郭英男夫婦身著阿美族傳統服飾入場，全場騷動，鎂光燈閃個不停，畢竟年邁的原住民唱者對上了全球矚目的奧運國際賽事與知名唱片公司，台灣原住民又是被侵權的一方，社會各界莫不將焦點放在這對老夫婦身上，亟欲了解郭英男夫婦目前的心情、立場與最後決定。

喧鬧的記者會場，在 Landy 低沉嗓音開始說明事件緣由之際，立刻轉為寂靜無聲，直到介紹郭英男夫婦時，現場爆出熱烈掌聲。郭英男靦腆地起身表示，很開心得悉這首曲子躍上國際舞台，可是覺得很奇怪，竟然沒有人知道這首歌是他演唱的，在滾石及魔岩唱片公司支持下，他決定向奧運侵權者討公道，讓全世界知道〈歡樂飲酒歌〉的歌聲來自台東的阿美族。

Landy 熟練地接過麥克風，簡單扼要地分析這個事件的重大疑點及音樂人、原住民的期許後，再將麥克風遞給我，以律師身分補充即將採取的法律程序——寄發律師函要求奧委會與 EMI 唱片公開道歉，承認侵權，並且回復原唱者之名聲及賠償損害。接下來郭英男夫婦及馬蘭吟唱隊的現場演唱，將記者會的會場氣氛引爆到最高點，高亢歡樂的歌聲結束之際，Landy 及時宣布記者會到此為止，畫上圓滿的句點。

正式委託美國律師發函警告

滾石高層在這段期間，強烈感受到郭英男夫婦及部落的殷殷期待，同時慮及唱片公司保護藝人權益及原住民音樂的立場。因此記者會前已積極落實法律行動，第一步是委託美國 Deway Ballantine 律師事務所撰擬律師函，敘述郭英男夫婦演唱〈歡樂飲酒歌〉遭受法國文化之家與謎樂團侵權經過，要求合理補償。律師函草稿經過我們反覆討論確認定稿後，正本於民國八十五年七月十八日寄予英國 EMI 唱片公司、德國瑪寶公司，副本發給奧委會、法國文化之家。

EMI 公司接獲律師函後，轉請謎樂團專輯唱片的製作公司——維京公司的律師 Bernard J. Fischbach 在美國時間七月二十六日（週四）致電予我方美國律師 Kelly C. Crabb，表示 EMI 公司已接獲郭英男的律師函，旋即詢問關於謎樂團使用〈歡樂飲酒歌〉之歌曲，並不是 X 教授於一九八八年郭英男在法國文化之家現場表演時錄音取得，而是 X 教授於一九六六年錄製提供一事，有何回應？維京唱片的律師先採取否認侵權的立場，認為歌曲錄音的權利在 X 教授手裡，謎樂團專輯使用的歌曲與郭英男夫婦無關，企圖卸免侵權責任。不過談話結束前，他還是好奇地問了一句話：「郭英男想要什麼？」我方委任的美國律師把問題轉回台灣，詢問我們郭英男夫婦的和解條件是什麼？

EMI 唱片公司對於我方遞出的侵權警告函有了回應，滾石唱片高層與郭英男夫婦都很振奮。在國內媒體一面倒的低迷氣氛中，維京唱片律師的來電不啻給我們一劑強心針，表示對方重視這份跨國的法律警告。縱使他們的律師在電話中流露出國際唱片公司的強勢與傲慢，不過，他們也不敢輕忽這樁可能演變為國際訴訟的侵權案，尤其是歌曲授權使用的對象是亞特蘭大奧運委員會。在奧運史上首次爆發宣傳曲侵權爭議，爆發的時機又正巧是四年一度的奧運賽事如火如荼進行中，奧委會的焦慮與持續施加在授權單位——EMI 唱片公司的壓力可想而知，難怪 EMI 唱片公司要求維京唱片的律師親自來電解釋，進一步想知道這對原住民夫婦的要求。

EMI 唱片公司詢問和解訴求

既然對方拋出問題，我們就得給答案，權利人被侵害時，首要的訴求當然是「正名」，侵權者必須要承認真正的權利人是何人，並且昭告天下。

因此，在我與滾石高層內部討論和解條件的會議中，第一項通過的共識就是 EMI 唱片公司與奧運委員會必須公開宣示〈歡樂飲酒歌〉演唱者是台東阿美族原住民郭英男夫婦，同時對於未經郭氏夫婦同意，擅自使用他們的歌聲，必須表達歉意。

權利人的尊嚴保住了之後，接下來要討論實質的損失，這個議題就涉及著作財產權的侵害，因而產生唱片版稅及授權金的損失，以及著作人格權的侵害衍生的精神上損害。通常侵害著作權造成的精神上損害，法律不會具體規定，被害人無法從著作權法條文找到具體金額的根據。因此我建議滾石唱片決策核心，先考慮著作財產權的經濟損失，這類著作權與授權金的計算，屬於唱片公司較為熟悉的財務模式，滾石唱片較能掌握相關數據。不過，面對國際唱片公司全球性的行銷實況，大家仍有疑惑……

「律師，我們對於 CD 售價、藝人版稅比例都瞭如指掌沒錯，可是EMI 唱片究竟在《徘徊不定》這張專輯銷售過程獲利多少？銷售總數量是幾張？還有他們授權〈返璞歸真〉這首歌曲給奧委會所收取的授權金，我們現在都無法得到精確的數據，要怎麼算出求償的金額呢？」魔岩唱片總經理在大家熱烈討論賠償項目之際，提出關鍵的問題。確實這些數據不明，將造成求償計算的瓶頸，財務長接著問：「我們可以要求 EMI 唱片公司提出這些數據或授權合約嗎？」

「恐怕很難，維京律師的態度急於撇清侵權責任，怎麼可能主動提供EMI 公司商業機密與財務收入？唯一可以得到這些數據金額的合法管道，只能透過法院發動調查權。可是目前還沒進入訴訟階段，無從啟動司法調查審計機制，倒是有位熱心的《中國郵報》（The China Post）記者鍥而不捨地追蹤這個案子，她寫信問了 EMI 唱片公司的高層，經理告訴她這張專輯在全球已經賣了五百萬張，也許我們可以用這個銷售量作為推算演唱者版稅的基礎。」我找出《中國郵報》記者傳真給我的信件交給財務長，一邊解釋法律程序。

歌曲版稅損失的計算

財務部門主管邊看信函，邊拿 CD 確認曲數說道：「一張 CD 如果售價是台幣二百五十元，共有九首曲子，暫時先以十首整除，再以百分之二十的藝人演唱版稅計算，藝人每張 CD 可以拿到五塊，五百萬張的全球銷售量，可以作為求償的版稅，而且還應該加上著作人格權的精神賠償跟奧運的授權金。我們的計算基礎這樣合理嗎？」財務長想確認計算公式是否可行。

「我想在美國音樂工業，歌手的版稅應該無法給到這麼高的比例，百分之二十真的很高，這一部分可能要再確認。」我提醒和解金的計算要符合唱片行業的商業模式，勿太樂觀。

「而且〈返璞歸真〉這首曲子一半是謎樂團的歌聲，郭英男夫妻演唱的部分大約只占一半，因此歌手版稅必須再折半。」魔岩總經理 Landy 再挑出另一個計算版稅的重點。於是大家再重新檢閱專輯 CD 及權利項目，以及美國律師提供的藝人可以求償的細項信函。

會議持續兩、三個小時後，我作了初步結論：「根據郭英男夫婦在這張謎樂團製作的專輯所享有的〈返璞歸真〉歌曲的權利，包括編曲的音樂著作權及演唱〈歡樂飲酒歌〉的表演著作權，擁有版稅比例為十八分之一（曲數九分之一乘以歌曲比例二分之一等於十八分之一），以這個比例計算銷售版稅及授權金，具體金額請美國律師調查《徘徊不定》專輯唱片銷售量，依照美國唱片公播規定，算出求償數據，以及要求日後專輯繼續發行的版稅支付方式與專輯署名。」

會後我將會議結論轉告美國律師後，美國律師允諾透過管道查訪《徘徊不定》專輯銷售數據，同時著手撰擬和解條件的信函手稿。一週後滾石唱片的高層再三審閱美國律師的和解求償信函後，確認內容無誤，通知我轉告美國律師於翌日（八月一日）將求償和解信函傳真予維京唱片的律師，接下來又得沉住氣等候對方的回音了。

五 EMI 唱片公司拒絕賠償

經過整整兩週的等待，我方委託的美國律師終於傳來消息說：「今天（八月十四日）我與維京唱片的律師協商，他們提出質疑，認為郭英男的〈歡樂飲酒歌〉是一九六六年在台灣錄製，一九七九年唱片在台灣發行；而一九六六年台灣並無世界各國承認的著作權法，郭英男的歌曲錄音不受美國保護，因此 EMI 唱片公司無須賠償。」

沒想到等待的結果，居然獲得如此不負責任的答覆，滾石唱片高層與我均感憤怒與憂心，覺得此樁侵權案的談判恐怕困難重重。但是對方的質疑又不能不回應，於是我盡快查閱相關資料後，向我方委託的美國律師說明以下重點：

1. 謎樂團的專輯中郭英男夫婦的歌聲是一九八八年錄製，在法國發行的《台灣原住民之複音歌唱》專輯內頁說明書載明〈歡樂飲酒歌〉是一九八八年在法國錄製。

2. 如果 EMI 唱片堅持是在一九六六年錄音，應該舉證。

3. 台灣一九二八年已制定有著作權法，一九四六年中美通商友好協定中明確規定著作權保護的互惠原則，一九九三年的中美協定第四條也明定台灣人民的著作權在美國亦受到保護，保護期可以追溯到一九六五年，因此不論是一九六六年或一九八八年的錄音，郭英男夫婦演唱的歌曲在美國都應該受到保護。

美國律師獲悉後找到相關規定，過兩天立即將這些重點以書面回覆予維京唱片的律師。詎知維京律師研究一週後回電，居然強調一九九三年的中美協定不能拘束美國，這個答覆真是匪夷所思，幸好翌日（八月二十三日）我方美國律師就列舉美國法院的案例支持中美協定的效力及於美國，美國必須遵守協定的內容，並且以書面向維京唱片的律師解釋。沉寂了十日後，維京唱片的律師才回覆，表示將與 EMI 唱片公司討論後，再作決定。

國內提出法律追訴程序

在焦灼等待美國和解談判回音的同時，台灣的法律追訴動作也同步展開，我代表郭英男夫婦在七月十八日寄發律師函予中國電視台及 TVBS 電視台，主要強調法國文化之家未徵得郭英男夫婦的同意，將其演唱之歌曲〈歡樂飲酒歌〉錄製為鐳射唱片，不僅未在該鐳射唱片上註明郭英男夫婦為演唱者之字樣，甚且事後擅自授權德國謎合唱團唱片公司收錄於《徘徊不定》專輯，該專輯亦未註明演唱者姓名，更未支付權利金，近日一九九六年亞特蘭大夏季奧運會選錄為宣傳短片歌曲，一再侵害著作人格權及財產權，電視台未經郭英男夫婦之授權，於晚間新聞奧運特別報導中持續播送〈歡樂飲酒歌〉之樂曲，有侵害郭英男夫婦著作權之嫌。籲請電視台盡速提出合法授權之相關文件，如涉有侵權情事，則應出面澄清處理。

十天後中國電視台指派主管來到我的事務所協商和解事宜，中視提出和解建議，希望雙方能簽訂和解書及〈歡樂飲酒歌〉的歌曲使用同意書，中視願意為郭英男製作播映特別節目。我趕緊將此和解條件轉達給滾石唱片，由魔岩的總經理向郭英男夫婦解釋。在美國和解談判陷於膠著之時，中視積極出面商談，我們都希望能達成和解，由侵權單位承認錯誤並致歉，讓我們持有一份註明〈歡樂飲酒歌〉權利人是郭英男夫婦的文件，這將會為低迷的侵權案注入強心劑。

沒料到唱片公司將中視的和解案件轉知當事人後，郭英男夫婦與家人不知何故商量多日，遲至八月八日始同意和解，中視獲悉後，認為亞特蘭大奧運業已閉幕，此時和解已無實益，故婉言回絕。我們接到此訊息，頗感錯愕，但也無奈，僅得另外冀望 TVBS 電視台能善意回應，孰料八月十九日 TVBS 委託律師回函表示：「奧委會聲稱亞特蘭大奧運的宣傳曲使用〈歡樂飲酒歌〉曾獲得合法授權，並無侵權疑義，如郭英男夫婦主張享有〈歡樂飲酒歌〉的著作權，應該要提出權利證明。」

國內電視台拒絕和解

顯然電視台根本不相信郭英男是〈歡樂飲酒歌〉的權利人！明明是郭英男夫婦演唱的歌曲，全世界都否認不了，可是一旦進入法律程序，就需要種種證據方法來證明權利的存在，這是文明世界設定的遊戲規則，不是一個原住民所能理解或做到的。倘使郭英男沒有與唱片公司簽約，唱片公司沒有委託律師團隊接案，恐怕到現在還沒有人知曉曾經有一張在美國告示排行榜 Billboard 蟬聯三十二週前一百名，全球銷售量逾五百萬張的專輯唱片中有一首主打歌一半是台灣阿美族的原住民演唱的。

可是縱令中、美律師攜手合作，提出侵權賠償的訴求，目前客觀局勢都對我們不利，除了專輯 CD 的歌聲可以透過鑑定確認是郭英男夫婦的原音外，所有的人證、物證、書證都無法作為郭英男擁有〈歡樂飲酒歌〉權利的依據，難怪國內、外侵權單位有恃無恐地陸續宣稱使用歌曲業經合法授權，拒絕和解。最初聽聞奧委會委員吳經國報告亞特蘭大奧運宣傳曲使用原住民郭英男的歌聲，奧運主席薩瑪蘭奇於七月十七日立刻裁示以奧委會名義發函向郭英男夫婦致敬，併表謝忱；但在翌日收到郭英男委託的美國律師寄發侵權警示的律師函之後，奧委會改口表示俟全案法律程序結束始表明立場。

想必奧委會認為全案係遭受池魚之殃所致，否則在奧運宣傳曲播出之前，已經依法向唱片發行公司 EMI 取得授權，怎麼事後又被扣上「侵權」的罪名？奧委會收到律師函之後，當然要求授權者──EMI 唱片公司出面交代，因此眼前侵權案能否和平解決的關鍵，端在 EMI 唱片公司的態度與立場。

在歷經國內播放侵權歌曲的中視、TVBS 電視台拒絕和解，加上奧委會改變和善的態度後，我們也在屏息等待 EMI 律師的回覆。從七月底、八月中旬到九月初的聯繫、溝通、解釋，維京唱片的律師就藉辭要與 EMI 公司商議，開始神隱。經過一個月音訊杳然，我們要求美國律師十月三日直接電詢 EMI 英國發行公司，電話中對方允諾一週後德國瑪寶製作公司指示律師具體回應，但期限屆至後卻石沉大海，於是十月八日我方的美國律師發函催促維京唱片盡速回覆。遲至美國感恩節前夕，EMI 唱片公司之委託律師竟以 EMI 唱片公司並未侵權，以及貧窮的原住民郭英男無力在美國打一樁可能耗資高達美金一百萬元的侵權官司為由，悍然拒絕和解。

股股期盼了四個月，非但和解談判破裂，對方甚至以如此輕蔑侮辱之字眼作為其被發現盜用著作之回應。郭英男得悉此一噩耗後，失望之餘，十分不解，為何法律支持他的立場，對方侵權後，卻仍如此跋扈，不肯認錯？他一輩子未進過法院、打過官司，無法理解犯錯的人常常是要到最後關頭才會低頭面對法律的制裁。郭英男天真地以為，今天我們提出抗議，明天對方就會致歉改過。

在歷經四個月的侵權案引爆、發函警告、談判協商、和解破裂之後，提告與否，滾石與魔岩唱片陷入兩難，數度召開會議深入討論及評估。當我再度前往魔岩唱片開會，在深切關心本案的魔岩唱片負責人段鍾潭、總經理張培仁面前，詳細分析美國法院的訴訟程序，及可能耗費的時間、金錢、人力後，本案的主角郭英男沉默了，他沒有想到正義的爭取、權利的維護竟要付出這麼大的代價……

決定向國際唱片公司宣戰

魔岩唱片看到郭英男眼中的渴望、語氣中的堅持，在公司經過數日的密集討論評估，最終為了維護原住民的音樂與郭英男的著作權，決定不計代價為改變台灣之形象、維護阿美族之尊嚴、爭取郭英男夫婦之權益，全力支持郭氏夫婦勇敢地跨出第一步，向國際唱片公司宣戰——進入美國法院提告，希望打一場漂亮的國際侵權法律戰。

接下來要正式部署戰局、選定訴訟律師、決定起訴法院及提求侵權求償的訴求。我先在台灣蒐集資料，篩選比較可能合作的律師事務所，在美國聖誕假期結束後，飛往美國與數家律師事務所接觸，詳細了解侵權訴訟的程序。美國律師先作出初步分析，如果郭英男夫婦提告侵權案，採取「簡易訴訟」的程序，只需歷經三個月的法院書面審理，毋需陪審團冗長的審判過程，全部費用為美金二十六萬元，但是採此途徑勝訴率不高，因為迄今為止，居於全案關鍵的Ｘ教授尚未表態與我方站在同一立場，而且EMI唱片公司矢口否認郭英男享有〈歡樂飲酒歌〉的著作權，因此走「簡易訴訟」的程序必然不能爭取勝訴結果。

另一個選項是進入美國法院「一般審判」程序，由於須經陪審團審判，估計官司至少耗時三年，律師費用高達美金八十五萬元，缺點是費用過高，而且曠日費時，當事人郭英男的年紀與體力恐怕無法負荷前往美國出庭或參加記者會，且扣除成本費用後，縱使勝訴，對方的賠償額度也所剩無幾。

但是好處是透過這樁空前的跨國訴訟，可以達到宣傳原住民音樂的目的，又能爭取郭英男的法律權益，而且勝訴時對方須負擔原告的合理訴訟及律師費，可以降低我方的成本費用。

跨國訴訟評估

我把這些評估因素及資訊帶回台灣後，引發滾石唱片決策核心的激烈討論，雖然大家都同意採取「一般審判」程序，但是律師費及相關費用——法律訴訟費一千元美金、證人口供取錄每人三千元美金、專家鑑定費（會計師計算 EMI 唱片的專輯收益、音樂專家比對侵權歌曲等）每人五千至兩萬元美金、審判翻譯費、交通車馬費、郵電影印等雜支，加總金額令人咋舌，當事人郭英男必然無力支付分毫，全部費用須仰賴滾石／魔岩唱片負

擔。因此滾石內部陷入長考，滾石老闆希望有其他付款方式的選項，於是

詢問我有無分段支付律師費用的可能性，先支付定額較低的費用例如兩萬

至五萬元美金，俟我方勝訴再支付後酬（contingency）？

我再向美國律師事務所查詢，多數事務所拒絕，因為此案非常複雜，

不僅侵權地跨越亞洲（台灣）、歐洲（法國）、美洲（美國），歌曲使用

歷程及案情發展長達三十年——一九六六至一九九六年，牽涉三十年間各

國著作權法的變更及案情事實之難以掌握，加上被告是 EMI 唱片公司，勢

力龐大、人脈綿密，原告的律師打贏官司拿到後酬的機率極低，於是多數

接觸中的美國律師事務所放棄接案機會。後來有位華人律師提醒，選擇律

師事務所須先確定起訴的法院，如果決定在東岸起訴就不適宜找西岸的律

師；反之如果選定在洛杉磯起訴，就不宜委託紐約的律師接辦，否則不僅

交通費用增加，而且律師不熟悉當地法院的習慣與流程，會影響案件的進

行。

面對如此善意的律師，我把握機會進一步請教他如何確定起訴法院？

他不厭其煩地詳細分析：「這個侵權案被告是 EMI 唱片公司及奧委會，由於 EMI 唱片銷售侵權歌曲〈歡樂飲酒歌〉的專輯銷售範圍遍及全美，因此美國每一個州都可以起訴。不過因為原告是台灣人，又是原住民，倘使選擇比較保守的州，或是白人較多的州，譬如美東的紐約、波士頓、華盛頓，恐怕陪審團及法官都不具同理心，也不會特別同情郭英男的被害人遭遇。這種跨國的侵權案，最好要找移民較多、娛樂業發達、觀念較開放的州，例如加州，它的電影工業蓬勃發展，法院對於音樂產業比較熟悉，而且外國居民比例高，陪審團的成員也會包含外國人，可能比較同情台灣的原住民，這樣勝訴的機會就提高了。」

六　確定向美國洛杉磯聯邦地區法院起訴

確實有道理，我順勢請這位華人律師介紹加州洛杉磯的律師事務所，他欣然同意，立刻推薦曾經合作的法律事務所，強調他們擁有出色的智慧財產權部門的律師。在數度洽商後，這家事務所樂意以較低額度的訂金，以及搭配收取後酬的方式與我們合作，並且在很短的期間內提出案件訴訟程序的時程表，簡要整理後寄給我們：

1. 一九九七年一月三十一日前郭英男夫婦在美國洛杉磯聯邦地區法院起訴

　＊原告：郭英男、郭秀珠

　＊被告：EMI 唱片公司、亞特蘭大奧運籌備委員會

　　（謎樂團、維京唱片、瑪賓音樂、法國文化之家將相繼在訴訟

中被 EMI 牽連為被告）

*訴求：(1)賠償過去合理損失（起訴時無法精確估算，須在訴訟中委託會計師向 EMI 財務部門索取全部報表資料鑑定）。

(2)支付未來合理版稅收入。

(3)更正著作人姓名。

2.被告 EMI、亞特蘭大奧委會須針對原告的起訴狀提出答辯。

3.聯邦地區法院接著將要求原告、被告在起訴之日起六十日內交換所得相關文件資料（ex.法國文化之家與謎樂團簽訂之授權合約，維京唱片與 EMI 簽訂之發行合約，EMI 公司之版稅報表）。

4.法院進行發現真實程序（discovery）原告、被告可要求證人作「口供取錄」之程序。EMI 可能要求原告郭英男、相關證人前往美國作證。

5.法院強制和解，和解不成則進入辯論、陪審團聽審程序，最後達成判決。

美國律師還預估從第一項至第五項須耗時三年。在審慎長考後，滾石唱片決定與他們合作，正式委託在加州法院開啟訴訟。

研究台灣著作權法歷年立法沿革

本來以為一旦委託美國的律師接辦此案，開始要提告，向法院起訴，我在台灣的法律支援工作會減少，沒想到不減反增。因為在美國打侵害著作權的官司，必須先在美國協會辦理著作權註冊登記，才能到法院起訴，於是我得在台灣先準備〈歡樂飲酒歌〉的基本資料及郭英男演唱的檔案，全部翻譯成英文，提供給美國律師代為申請著作權登記，這個註冊手續就耗費將近半年。

此外，美國律師要求我研究台灣一九六六年起至起訴的著作權法的立法沿革及各次變更的法條內容，並且對應到這個侵權案件重要時間點一九六六年 X 教授田野採集、一九七九年台北第一唱片錄音、一九八八年法國文化之家表演、一九九四年 EMI 唱片發行專輯、一九九六年美國奧運侵權的各階段台灣著作權法的相關規定。尤其是針對我方主張侵權的編曲音樂著作權及表演著作權之法律依據，以及著作權法主管機關的意見。於是我將立法院相關資料詳細研讀、一一臚列，再佐以文字分析說明，撰擬完成一份厚厚的法律意見書。

孰知擬就這份文件之後，美國律師認為還不足以證明郭英男享有編曲音樂著作權，我只好請教美國律師要提出怎樣的證據，法官才能相信郭英男曾經針對〈歡樂飲酒歌〉重新編曲？美國律師的答案令人傻眼，他要求提出的證據方法，簡直是強人所難，聽完他的回覆，我真想放棄了！

查證〈歡樂飲酒歌〉原版旋律

美國律師說：「請妳找出幾十年前郭英男改編後的版本，讓法官比對是否改編程度高達百分之八十以上，而且這兩份版本比對的檔案要提交到法庭之前，請妳找到台灣的專家鑑定人，鑑定兩個版本的異同，再加註相對應著作權法的法律意見，提出英文版的法律意見書。這份法律意見書不適宜由妳或我撰擬，因為法官需要第三方的專家意見，我們都是郭英男的委託律師，寫出來的法律意見書公信力不足，陪審團也不會採納的。」

幾十年前改編的歌曲版本到哪兒去找呢？我們哪知道郭英男改編前長年流傳於部落的〈歡樂飲酒歌〉旋律為何呢？我們只是聽過部落耆老及郭英男提過這個故事，而且約略哼出原版的旋律而已，要怎麼去找到幾十年前的原版歌聲呢？這項不可能的任務怎麼達成呢？萬般苦惱之下，我還是得接下這個艱難的任務，同時向滾石唱片求助，期待他們能找到歷史檔案。

魔岩唱片公司人員直接飛到台東，上窮碧落下黃泉，四處向部落打探歷史資料，動員許多族人翻箱倒櫃，翻遍整個部落，居然不負所託，找到幾十年前的〈歡樂飲酒歌〉老版本，當時稱為〈第二首長歌〉。我們比對郭英男改編後的版本，確實已有八成以上的改變，顯然能夠證實我們提出郭英男擁有編曲之音樂著作權的主張。

委託法學教授撰擬法律意見書

可是這種版本比對的結果不是我們說了算，美國律師知道有這個結果之後，興奮之情溢於言表，但仍提議由專家證人來進行比對、分析，作成書面意見。到底要怎樣的人選才能符合這個需求呢？雖然旋律的差異一聽即知，可是要把這份差異對應到相關著作權法規定，整理出台灣著作權法近三十年來的沿革變更，恐怕只有法學者可以勝任，於是我回到母校討救兵。昔日台大法研所的學長謝銘洋在德國攻讀法學博士後，回到台灣大學法律系任教（現任大法官），專攻智慧財產法，著作權相關的著作豐富，講學著述在國內頗受好評。我把謝銘洋教授的職經歷傳真給美國律師後，他們認為謝教授的資歷日後擔任侵權訴訟案的專家證人無可挑剔，因此請我先委託謝教授撰擬法律意見書，作為侵權案提告的準備。

我把不同版本的〈歡樂飲酒歌〉錄音帶，以及侵權案的三張專輯CD，包括第一唱片公司的《阿美族民歌》、法國文化之家的《台灣原住民複音歌唱》與EMI唱片一九九四年發行的《徘徊不定》專輯一起帶著，前往台大法學院拜訪謝銘洋教授。由於事前在電話裡已經說明案情梗概，謝教授完全掌握事實背景及案情資料，於是我們在教師休息室一見面就播放〈歡樂飲酒歌〉新舊版本，謝教授反覆聽了幾次，確定新版本的歌曲已經修改百分之八十以上的旋律。繼之討論此案在台灣、美國、法國的侵權要件，以及EMI唱片與奧委會應該承擔的賠償法律責任，在確立這些被告的侵權責任後，謝教授欣然接受這項委託，允諾一個月內完成中、英文版的法律意見書。

再準備侵權案文件，包含我整理的案情分析、事實經過與法律意見，前往

郭英男夫婦起訴

　　在一切起訴文件備齊後，郭英男夫婦透過滾石／魔岩唱片的支持協助，以及我的安排，委託美國律師向加州中央地區法院遞交起訴狀，起訴狀首頁載明，原告是郭英男郭秀珠，被告包括維京唱片公司、瑪寶音樂公司、克里斯瑪唱片、EMI 唱片公司、謎樂團、製作人克里圖、國際奧林匹克運動委員會，案號為 97-9602 JSL（AIJX），訴請侵害著作權之損害賠償，而且特別註明需要陪審團，起訴狀內容重點如後：

1. 根據一九七六年著作權法，美國法典第十七篇第一○一條及其以下之規定，此係一侵害著作權之訴訟。

2. 依美國法典第二十八篇第一三三一條、一三三八條（a）和（b）項及其補充管轄權，此訴訟係隸屬於此法院所管轄。

3. 原告郭英男和郭秀珠為夫妻，係一音樂作品之著作人、音樂著作之表演人及於中華民國台灣省台東市豐谷北路所錄製之音樂錄音物之製作人。

4. 原告聲稱一九九二年十二月後，被告等分別故意暨直接地侵害原告之歌之著作權，包括實際地抄襲、公開地演出、製作暨製作及散布、參與並助長如此之侵權行為或分得所有藉由實際地使用原告之歌於被告克里圖和謎樂團錄製之〈返璞歸真〉一曲及作為此曲之一部所得之收益。

5. 〈返璞歸真〉一曲後以單曲之形式呈現並收錄於《徘徊不定》專輯。

6. 被告克里圖、謎樂團和瑪寶音樂公司參與並促成重製原告之歌以創作及錄製〈返璞歸真〉一曲。

7. 被告瑪寶音樂公司、克里斯瑪唱片、EMI唱片及維京唱片公司促成暨參與製造並散布用於機械上重製〈返璞歸真〉一曲之有聲錄音物於美國及世界各國。

8. 被告奧委會、克里圖及謎樂團促成暨參與謎樂團公開演出〈返璞歸真〉一事。

9. 奧委會特別使用原告之歌於一九九六年奧運會之宣傳短片中。

10. 原告等係於一九九六年始知悉被告等直接侵害原告等之國際著作權之違法行為。

11. 被告等因未分別地於相關之有聲出版物說明書中將原告之歌之來源及著作權之所有權歸屬於原告等，而製造了一個關於原告之歌曲及其錄音物錯誤來源的印象。

12. 原告等未獲得法律上應有之補償，且上述錯誤之說明書已造成且將繼續造成原告無法彌補之傷害暨損失。據此，原告等主張其個別之請求：

(1) 訴訟未決期間暨永久地禁止被告等個人、其各個代理人、受僱人及代表人以任何形式侵害原告等之著作權，包括銷售、製造、散布被告克里圖與謎樂團所錄製之〈返璞歸真〉錄音物暨授權、促成參與及助長任何之侵權行為。

(2)命令被告等每人結算由渠等之每一著作侵權行為所生之所有營利、收益暨利益，並給付原告等因每一侵害上述著作權之行為所遭受之損害賠償金額或法院就著作權法規定之適當範圍內所判之損害賠償金額。

(3)命令被告等每人宣誓交付於訴訟未決期間及為銷燬所扣押之所有侵權複製品、錄音物、有聲錄音物暨所有金屬版、板模、鑄作物及任何其他製造侵權錄音物、有聲錄音物複製品之工具。

(4)被告等應給付原告等此訴訟之費用包括法院允許原告等得請求之適度之律師費用。

(5)原告等應得其餘暨後續之補償。

七　美國加州法院受理侵權案

戰鼓鳴起，台灣原住民向國際唱片宣戰，且看美國法院如何面對這樁跨國侵權訴訟了。加州法院受理此案後，要求原告將起訴狀繕本送給每一位被告，包括 EMI 唱片公司、維京唱片公司、瑪寶音樂公司、製作人克里圖、謎樂團、奧委會。

起訴十日後，承審法官 J. Spencer Letts 代表法院通知原告與被告兩造，〈歡樂飲酒歌〉侵權案由他承辦，被告應該在收到原告送達的起訴狀後三十天內提出答辯狀，繼而雙方律師應在律師事務所進行強制性的非正式會議，討論此案的審判準備事項。

美國訴訟制度與台灣法院實務有極多地方不同，以起訴狀送達為例，在台灣的法院提起民事訴訟時，只要把起訴狀正本及依被告人數準備的繕本份數同時交給法院收發處，原告的責任已盡，接下來只需等候法院通知，送達起訴狀的責任完全由法院承擔。法官要負責把起訴狀寄達給每一位被告，萬一原告起訴狀上提供的被告地址送達不到，法官再通知原告另行呈送被告戶籍地或公司營業所，或以公示送達的程序代之。但在美國法院則必須由原告自行負責將起訴狀送交到每一位被告手上，並且須有送達的證明。倘若雙方對於書狀送達發生爭議，原告必須提供送達員的證詞或物證，用來證明已盡到起訴狀送達的義務。

這個侵權案我方律師在訴訟程序中，首度遭遇的問題就是起訴狀送達的困難。被告之中公司法人包括奧委會、EMI唱片公司、維京唱片、瑪寶音樂、克里斯瑪唱片及謎樂團只經過一些時日的文書作業處理，就順利地送達起訴狀，但專輯製作人克里圖長時間外出，不住在居所地，送達員幾次都無法順利送達給他本人，後來美國律師不得已，在商請我們的同意後，特別僱請偵探查訪被告克里圖的現居所，才查知克里圖剛巧在這幾個月前往地中海上一個小島旅行兼出差工作，出沒不定，偵探花了好大的力氣才帶領送達員成功地將起訴狀面交給小島上的克里圖本人，完成起訴狀送達任務。當然這筆額外的偵探費及搭機／船到小島的交通費又得由我方支付，這些意外的支出日後不斷地出現，滾石唱片事到臨頭也得咬緊牙關地概括承受，全面買單了。

被告 EMI 唱片在民國八十七年一月二十日收到起訴狀，二月九日就委託律師史密斯（Joel Mocabe Smith）來函告知我方郭英男夫婦訴之美國章均寧律師（Emil C. Chang），聲明他代表被告進行本案訴訟，將於二月十九日提出答辯狀，並詢問 EMI 及維京唱片公司送達情形。章均寧律師在二月十二日回信，提醒史密斯律師此案備受國際矚目，隨著案件之訴訟進展，對於被告之負面批評聲浪也將接踵而至，被告律師團宜有心理準備。

章律師除了代表郭英男夫婦處理侵權案的訴訟程序之外，還寄發「爭議通知書」到美國著作權登記機關 ASCAP，要求提供侵權案歌曲〈返璞歸真〉應支付的所有權利金明細。此外，我們考慮郭英男夫婦預備在法國向法國文化之家及其他發行〈返璞歸真〉歌曲的公司提告，章律師也同步聯繫其事務所之法國合作律師 Therese de Saint Palle，委託研究本案在法國訴訟的可行性，及查明法國文化之家的組織性質、創立時間、目的、經費來源。

同步委託律師研究在法國訴訟的可行性

Palle 律師研究案情後，提出一連串疑問，我方章律師於二月十九日回覆如後：

1. 郭英男夫婦對於 X 教授錄製之專輯或法國文化之家製作之 CD 皆不知情，亦未針對其後被告等所發行之錄音著作物為任何口頭或書面之授權。

章律師同時以書面答覆法國律師的助理 Alexandra 之問題：

1. X 教授於一九七八年與郭氏夫婦接觸並錄製了一品質不佳之錄音著作物，後其基於錄音效果之考量，乃製作了一九七九年之錄音物。法國文化之家所使用者即係一九七九年之錄音物。

2. X 教授製作前揭錄音物可能係代表 X 藝術基金會所為。我方並未擁有前揭收錄被侵權曲〈歡樂飲酒歌〉之錄音物。

3. 根據過去十八個月來之調查，我方並未發現郭氏夫婦所簽署之任何書面

2. 除就法國文化之家外，我方亦有意控告法國文化之家、EMI 唱片及維京公司。

3. 已要求律師考慮對台灣 EMI 起訴或發律師函，使此案於世界各國之訴訟同時進行以促進此案盡早圓滿之解決。

授權文件，關於此點將再向律師確認。

4. 此案系爭歌曲僅係〈歡樂飲酒歌〉，將寄一卷此原曲之拷貝帶予 Alexandra。

承審法官強烈要求和解

同一時間加州法院的法官 Letts 也有動作了，法官決定一九九八年四月一日召開「準備會議（status conference）」，雙方律師接到傳票後，如期出席會議。會議開始法官一坐定就疾言厲色地向被告們諭示：「我絕不允許這麼複雜的案子進入我的法庭，接受大陪審團的審判，你們必須立刻商談和解。」被告公司委託律師默不回應，在兩造依程序陳述各自主張後，法官指示雙方在兩週內交換書狀，說明事實及提出相關書狀。

我方律師章均寧在五天後立即以信函通知 EMI 公司委託的史密斯律師，表明：「1. 原告對於合理的和解條件保持開放的立場，如需進一步討論和解事宜，我隨時願意配合；2.你們所聘請的中國律師提到郭英男夫婦的〈歡樂飲酒歌〉一九七九年錄製的版本在當時不受台灣著作權法保護的觀點是錯誤的，你們應該重新檢視所有法律的規定；3.尤其最值得注意的是在此案中你們所主張著作權已轉讓予被告公司的說辭是無法獲得台灣著作權法的支持。」

史密斯律師代表 EMI 唱片公司在同日（四月六日）立刻回信，針對我方章律師的前述告知完全不作回應，只是攻擊原告的傳票尚未合法送交全體被告，甚至從程序中否認加州中央地區法院對於此案擁有司法管轄權，企圖從程序的合法性推翻此案。他不懷好意地宣稱：「我完全看不出來被告維京唱片公司關於謎樂團〈返璞歸真〉歌曲與美國加州地區法院有何關聯性，請讓我知曉依據什麼行為或事實可以合理化原告在加州控告維京唱片的論點。」

到了四月十五日史密斯律師又寫了一封措詞強烈的信，除了抱怨我方律師尚未在兩週內依照法官的指示提出「事實、文件與證據」交付給被告，以至於被告的答辯狀需延期提出之外，還強調郭英男夫婦演唱的〈歡樂飲酒歌〉的著作權享有者的主張完全欠缺法律根據，甚至依被告的研究，在那段時期台灣的法律對於錄音帶（sound recordings）並無任何保護的規定。

維京唱片質疑原告立場

　　史密斯律師以示威性的口吻說：「案發當時美國的著作權法相關規定倒是非常明確，倘若你們找到台灣法律任何可以支持原告論點的條文，願意提供給我們參考，我們會倍覺感激！一旦你們可以提出 Letts 法官所要求的有力事實與證據，我們被告一定會照法官庭諭，立刻回應。」最後史密斯再次強調維京音樂公司在美國加州並沒有參與任何實質經濟活動，加州法院對維京音樂欠缺司法管轄權，郭英男夫婦不應該對維京唱片提告。

　　史密斯律師的信函字裡行間充滿倨傲與挑釁，不斷抬出 Letts 法官的名義，企圖施加壓力，迫使我方提供更多訴訟資訊。章均寧律師緊急與台灣的我們透過電話、傳真信函及電子郵件密集協商後，在四月二十三日嚴肅凌厲地回應密斯律師的信。

信函首段就抗議被告的主張——郭英男夫婦的歌曲著作權不受法律保護，認為被告這種立場是不符事實，也不合法。接下來指出四月一日的庭訊中，我方已詳細分析解釋郭英男改編〈歡樂飲酒歌〉的旋律，新舊版本大相逕庭，有證人可以證實。並且反過來要求被告，如果堅持郭英男的歌曲屬於公共財（Public domain），應該同步提出證據，包括人證與物證。

章律師信心堅定地答覆：「我們研究這個案子超過一年，發現沒有任何證據支持郭英男演唱的〈歡樂飲酒歌〉是公共財，所有我們準備的證據都指向郭英男擁有全部的著作權，這是無庸置疑的。為了協助你們了解台灣的著作權法，於茲說明台灣著作權法曾在一九六四、一九八五、一九九〇、一九九二的六月及七月、一九九三年都曾修法，一九六四年的版本規定著作權受到一些限制，但是到了一九八五年大幅度修法頒布後，還規定可以追溯適用，依據第三章第十三、十四、二十四、二十七、二十九、三十一條（Article 三．Sections 十三等）擴大著作權法的保護，盡量讓台灣之著作權法與《伯恩公約》（Berne Convention）一致，因此郭英男擁有〈歡樂飲酒歌〉的著作權是有法律依據的，倘使被告仍堅持相反的論點，請提供特定理由及法律規定加以說明。」

至於維京音樂的司法管轄權之訴求，章律師只以「等你正式取得維京音樂的訴訟代理委託，再來跟我談吧！」四兩撥千斤地回應了。同時要求被告提出下列資料：

1. 被告克里圖（製作人）的現今居所地。
2. 史密斯律師與維京音樂之關係。
3. 其他哪些被告主張〈返璞歸真〉的著作權。

4. 被告主張〈歡樂飲酒歌〉是公共財的法律基礎。

5. 〈返璞歸真〉歌曲在美國及其他地區銷售的收入來源及財務資料。

被告的律師挑釁回應

最後不忘提醒被告，希望他們能遵照法官的指示盡速針對本案作實質的答辯，勿再玩弄程序的技巧，那會是無濟於事，只是拖延訴訟而已！被告的律師史密斯收到這封嚴正聲明的信函後，不甘示弱，一週後也回覆一封充滿火藥味的信函，看來侵權案雙方的煙硝戰已經延燒到法庭外了。

史密斯律師在四月三十日回信中，不僅諷刺原告律師四月二十三日的信函對於案情的釐清毫無助益，無法提供被告理解為何郭英男演唱的歌曲擁有著作權，被告對於台灣著作權法深入研究，也完全掌握歷次修改的條文精神，但是這些修改與郭英男在本案擁有的權利有何關聯，還是無法獲得答案，因而有必要要求原告以書面回答下述問題：

1. 原告在本案中訴求的錄音是哪一年製作的？

2. 為何原告會演唱這首歌曲，錄製成錄音帶，有什麼情況促使他們錄音？

3. 原告質疑的這首歌曲的演唱錄音，是否沒有任何文件存在？

4. 原告主張一九八八年在法國文化之家表演時錄製的歌曲是有爭議的，這是原告所持的論點嗎？如果是的話，我方（被告）將提出明確的文件資料澄清這個爭議。

5. 原告主張侵權歌曲與成為公共財的〈歡樂飲酒歌〉有極大的差異，請提供明確的人證、物證讓我們查核。

史密斯律師在信中同時請求原告進一步解釋郭英男享有著作權的台灣著作權法依據，只要原告提得出來，被告一定能夠強有力地反駁。至於維京音樂的加州法院司法管轄權，被告毫無意圖要玩「程序遊戲」，如果有必要，雙方可能要回到法庭釐清這個重要議題，等到原告解釋清楚，被告維京音樂就可以決定是否委託律師處理此案了。章律師接獲這封極端不友善的信，雖然深感憤怒，認為被告只是推拖延宕，毫無解決侵權爭議的誠意；但也覺無奈，因為這種訴訟手法正是大財團面對訴訟常用的卑劣首段。

為了避免法官誤會，章律師決定蒐集更多維京音樂在加州針對侵權歌曲進行的經濟活動的諸多證據，於六月十五日正式遞出書狀向法官解釋。

史密斯律師獲悉後，怒不可遏，連忙在兩日後寫一封信譴責我方律師，而且以極為鄙夷的語氣，批評我方律師迄未針對被告數次提問具體答覆。

於是重複引述上一封信提出的問題，甚至加上結論指出，縱使郭英男主張的錄音帶享有受到台灣著作權法的保護，錄音歌曲的著作權也應該歸於 X 藝術基金會享有，郭英男依然沒有著作權，那麼提出這件侵權案有什麼法律根據呢？信末還激烈地表示，既然原告一直答非所問，雙方的交換書狀淪為被告扮演獨角戲，將向法官報告訴訟兩造已走入死胡同，無法交換書狀釐清案情，請求法院重啟調查，但最後願意再給原告一個補正的機會，如果十天內原告再不具體答覆上一封信的提問，被告將請法官回復本案的訴訟程序。

不過史密斯又不忘語帶玄機地附上一段被告關於和解的看法，他說：

「你們在六月十五日的書狀上表示和解的話，就不必再進入浪費司法資源的正式調查程序，被告也毋庸提出更多額外的資料，基於原告對於和解討論的渴求，我們認為這是很荒謬的建議！除非明天就是世界末日，不然我們怎麼可能面對原告無法證實他在本案的主張都是正確的，卻要求進入和解談判，這是前後顛倒的不合理的情節。假使原告期盼：提出一個和解的需求，我還是會跟被告們討論，對於本案進行評估，再提供和解的初步想法，如果你們有此堅持，就不必回覆我上述的疑問了。」

我們律師仔細研究被告最後這一封信，覺得很疑惑，被告的態度模稜兩可，表面上似乎很強硬地逼迫我方提出諸多事實證據，可是最終又不忘送上臨別秋波——和解的提議。究竟是被告拖延訴訟的策略，還是心虛企盼和解，令人費解，我與章律師商量的結果，認為這封信雖然語氣強勢，但真正用意我們仍須再三推敲，接下來是重啟和解談判，抑或回復法庭審判程序，端視承審法官的態度了。

我方律師在民國八十七年六月十五日遞出的書狀，點燃了〈歡樂飲酒歌〉訴訟的戰火，雙方真正要進入法庭攻防的肉搏戰。法官接著立即在七月十六日召開聽證程序，要求雙方以書面提出證人名單及證明的事項，同時必須摘要書寫證人的聲明書，互相交換資訊，作為審判的準備。被告律師立刻積極進行收編證人的工作，預備提交給加州法院的承審法官，列為審判庭傳訊的證人，這些檯面下暗自敲定的動作，我們事前完全無法探知，更無預防的可能，直到九月四日收到史密斯律師的信函，才知道被告謀略之強，用力之深！

被告證人名單猶如震撼彈

被告律師提交的證人名單，最具震撼力的莫過於台灣的民俗音樂學者X教授，被告希望透過X教授的證詞，證實一九七八年他到台東錄製郭英男夫婦演唱〈歡樂飲酒歌〉，錄音著作權屬於X教授所有，並且在郭英男夫婦於一九八八年前往法國文化之家表演後，X教授翌年因應法國文化之家之請求，以X藝術基金會之名義授權法國文化之家使用，共同發行《台灣原住民的複音歌唱》專輯。這個關卡只要打通了之後，法國文化之家授權EMI唱片使用，繼之再授權予奧委會，一連串原本侵權的違法行徑，一瞬間都翻轉為合法。此外，被告還列出台灣著作權法學者、法國文化之家職員、《中國新聞》的記者，將分別出庭證明台灣著作權法只保護錄製唱片者，法國文化之家獲得授權才使用〈歡樂飲酒歌〉郭英男夫婦的歌聲，以及郭英男夫婦早在一九九三年已經知悉EMI唱片公司使用他們的歌聲，藉此主張我方在一九九七年才提起訴訟，請求權時效業已消滅。

我們看到這份證人名單非常震驚，尤其看到 X 教授簽署的聲明書，更是難以置信，連忙與滾石唱片高層討論因應方案，同時電詢郭英男關於當年 X 教授錄製歌聲之經過。我將郭英男的說辭整理後傳真給章均寧律師，經過幾番電話、傳真信函往來後，我們發現這批被告既已勞師動眾，跨海尋求台灣的證人，且成功取得他們的允諾，勢必在法庭裡力戰到底，不可能輕易屈服。於是我們也作長期抗戰的準備，不僅增聘美國律師，加強律師團隊實力，並且於一九九九年一月十一日再追加侵權被告，包括 EMI 唱片轉授權的公司包括 AKA 製作公司、SONY 音樂集團、Warlock 唱片公司、電影公司等，合計十七家公司，成為侵權案第二波追訴對象，理由是 EMI 唱片使用〈歡樂飲酒歌〉並未獲得合法授權，EMI 轉授權的公司當然也構成侵權，追加這些重量級的被告也展現我們全力反擊的決心！

徹夜談判和解破局

雖然追加起訴的被告確實達到我們的策略目標──給予 EMI 唱片更大的壓力，迫使被告同意開啟第二輪調解會議。但是調解會議在雙方當事人、律師及保險公司持續六個小時的協商，而我在台灣徹夜守候，隨時通話討論下，依然功敗垂成，雙方各自提出的和解金額差距太大，和解終告破局。加州法院法官 Judge Ietts 確認兩造協商失敗，立刻訂下一九九九年七月十三日的審判庭，諭知原告郭英男夫婦必須出庭，在加州法院陪審團面前接受訊問。

沒想到起訴一年半之後，終究還是走到這一步，原告、被告雙方必須進入法庭接受審判，這是我們最不樂見的程序，它還是發生了。這時郭英男已經七十六歲了，體力大不如前，倘若一路從台灣飛到洛杉磯，我們真的沒把握經過飛機舟車勞頓之後，一旦步入法院，他能否頭腦清楚、鎮定如常地說明三十年前的事實？在這個巨大的出庭壓力之下，我與美國律師都密切討論，苦思良策，看看能否找出好方法，讓郭英男夫婦不用承受出庭審訊的煎熬，又能夠解決這樁愈來愈棘手的侵權案。

我苦苦思索了兩個月，深感時至今日，與其坐困愁城，不如拿出殺手鐧與對方生死對決了。於是我向滾石高層提出前往法國控告法國文化之家的訴訟策略，三年前侵權案爆發，之所以沒有考慮與加州法院同步起訴，是憂心訴訟戰線過長，勞民傷財，而且心中深盼美國的訴訟可以盡速和解，毋庸開啟多國訴訟，以免增加經濟、時間、人力的勞費支出，沒想到美國法院的被告盛氣凌人、頑抗不屈，甚至神通廣大，請來了台灣多位專家證人出庭背書作證，眼看侵權案對我方日益不利，我只好建議滾石唱片再闢戰場，背水一戰。

美國的章律師與我電話溝通後，心情沉重地在八十八年四月十九日的來信中，作成法國訴訟的利弊得失分析，建請我方當事人盡快作成決定，好讓他與法國律師趕在五月份向法國法院起訴，藉由法國文化之家一併成為侵權案被告的訴求，加上媒體壓力，逼迫 EMI 唱片出面談和。雖然這個策略極佳，而且也很可能達到我們設定的目標，可是多一條戰線畢竟又會增加人力、財務的負擔，因此滾石高層聽完我的分析後，猶豫再三，對於不熟悉外國司法制度的我們而言，打官司已是折騰，打外國官司更是辛苦，所以我也不忍心催促他們儘速定案，沉思三日後，滾石老闆請我詢問美國律師，可否以正式信函通知被告及法國文化之家，再給他們一次和解的機會，倘使三度和解依然破局，郭英男夫婦將在法國開啟侵權訴訟。

展開新一波的國際媒體宣傳與攻擊

　　美國章均寧律師對於這種試探性地放消息的手法，完全沒把握效果如何，不過為了滿足當事人的需求，他還是聯繫 EMI 唱片的史密斯律師，透露原告下一步即將採取的行動。史密斯律師不以為意地應允轉達這個訊息，我們都以為這種試探不足以發生多大效用，於是展開新一波的國際媒體宣傳與攻擊，沒想到一週後，卻有戲劇性的變化，EMI唱片居然釋出善意，同意雙方再坐下來，進行第三次談判。我們驚訝之餘，仍期盼奇蹟出現，如果和解能談成，我們就毋需心驚膽戰地帶著年邁的郭英男夫婦，飛往美國出席七月十三日加州法院的審判庭應訊了。

不過雙方要趕在七月十三日開庭前完成和解談判，的確是椿不可能的任務，在沉重的時間壓力下，美國律師立即安排協商的時間地點。然而為了預防和解破裂，原告必須遵照法官的提示出庭應訊。章律師建議我們必須同步與郭英男溝通各項問題，包括我方律師及對方律師可能的提問，務必一切回答符合我方立場，不能有任何閃失，尤其對於被告律師可能會緊追不捨，死纏爛打的問題，要反覆演練，讓郭英男熟悉法庭氣氛及對方逼問方式，免得在情緒被擾亂下，不慎說出對我方不利的答案。於是我一方面與滾石唱片深入討論和解條件，一方面請郭英男夫婦北上模擬演練各項法庭提問，整個五月份全部心力投入這個案件，全力戒備，等候美方消息。

八 EMI 唱片同意接受我方的和解條件

這一次的策略重點，一方面拉長戰線，向 EMI 唱片公司施壓，二方面引發國際媒體之注目。果然此項策略奏效，EMI 唱片公司承受不了轉授權公司挨告後持續強烈的反彈與抗議，以及可能加入法國被告的戰略，再度要求商談和解。經過數週艱苦的談判，終於在同年六月間傳來和解的捷報，EMI 唱片在其他眾多被告的壓力下，願意接受我方的和解條件，包括金錢賠償、支付版稅，承認〈歡樂飲酒歌〉的編曲音樂著作權及表演著作權為郭英男夫婦擁有，並且致贈兩張白金唱片，以示感謝他們的貢獻。

和解在即，郭英男先生卻陷入「接受和解或繼續審判」的疑惑與掙扎中，站在律師的立場，不能為當事人作成決定，只能分析利弊得失提供參考。經過數日的長考與家庭會議，郭英男先生親口告訴我，他同意和解，因為考量到 EMI 唱片公司提出的和解書中載明郭英男夫婦正式將〈歡樂飲酒歌〉追認授權予 EMI 唱片公司等使用，而且 EMI 唱片公司為感謝郭英男夫婦對專輯唱片的貢獻，承諾透過美國律師在八十八年十二月八日來台頒贈白金唱片予郭英男夫婦，並將在日後產製發行的鐳射唱片上標明〈返璞歸真〉一曲改編自台灣台東阿美族郭英男先生編曲、郭英男夫婦演唱之〈歡樂飲酒歌〉。

郭英男說他爭取尊重的訴訟目的達到了，而且阿美族天生喜好和平，在阿美族的音樂裡，只有包容、沒有對立，面對 EMI 唱片公司的歡意與誠意，他沒有理由不原諒對方。八十八年六月八日郭英男夫婦當著我及魔岩唱片總經理的面親筆簽下了和解書，結束了這場長達三年的國際侵權爭訟。

後記

這樁跨國訴訟案促成民國八十七年立法院通過著作權法增訂「表演著作」條文，之後於九十六年也催生了「原住民族傳統智慧創作條例」，後來更成為各大學法律系探討智慧財產權時的指標案例。

INK

Magic 29

〈歡樂飲酒歌〉國際侵權訴訟案
——台灣原住民vs.亞特蘭大奧運

Elders Drinking Song: International Litigation on Copyright Infringement
——Taiwan aboriginal vs. Atlanta Olympics

作 者	蘭天律師 Huang Shiu-Lan
總 編 輯	初安民 Chu An-Min
責 任 編 輯	宋敏菁 Sung Min-Ching
美 術 編 輯	黃昶憲 Jasper Huang 陳淑美 May Chen
校 對	黃秀蘭 Huang Shiu-Lan 丁天欣 Kara Plastich 凌孝於 Hsiao-Yu, Ling

發 行 人	張書銘
出 版	INK印刻文學生活雜誌出版股份有限公司
	新北市中和區建一路249號8樓
	電話：02-22281626
	傳眞：02-22281598
	e-mail：ink.book@msa.hinet.net
網 址	舒讀網http://www.inksudu.com.tw

法律顧問	巨鼎博達法律事務所
	施竣中律師
總 代 理	成陽出版股份有限公司
	電話：03-3589000（代表號）
	傳眞：03-3556521
郵政劃撥	19785090 印刻文學生活雜誌出版股份有限公司
印 刷	海王印刷事業股份有限公司

港澳總經銷	泛華發行代理有限公司
地 址	香港新界將軍澳工業邨駿昌街7號2樓
電 話	(852) 2798 2220
傳 眞	(852) 2796 5471
網 址	www.gccd.com.hk

出版日期	2023 年5月　初版
ISBN	978-986-387-652-6

定 價　400元

國家圖書館出版品預行編目資料

〈歡樂飲酒歌〉國際侵權訴訟案
——台灣原住民vs.亞特蘭大奧運／
蘭天律師 著.--初版, --新北市中和區：
INK印刻文學,
2023.05　面；公分（Magic；29）
ISBN 978-986-387-652-6（平裝）
1.著作權法 2.智慧財產權 3.國際侵權行為
588.34　　　　　112004937

舒讀網

"Elders Drinking Song" International Litigation on Copyright Infringement
Taiwan aboriginal vs. Atlanta Olympics

Huang Shiu-Lan

Content

Forward
How I Come to know Lawyer Huang Shiu Lan

Professor Emeritus of Taipei National
Universityof the Arts
Lee Daw Ming

Thanks to my trusty old friend Ms. Angelika Geng Yu Wang's introduction, in October 2017 I was able to invite Lawyer Huang Shiu Lan to give a speech on topics covering Intellectual Property & Licensing, Signing Contract and Avoiding the Traps, Insurance for Filmmakers and Productions for the junior and senior students in the Department of Filmmaking at Taipei National University of the Arts where I was teaching at the time.

The purpose was to resolve students' confusion and their concerns for issues related to intellectual property rights, especially those on securing the rights and permissions, how not to break the law, how to protect their work (scripts or films) from piracy, and what to watch out and how to avoid the traps upon signing the agreement in their role as an actor, a

screenwriter, or a director.

Considering TNUA is located in the hilly regions of Guandu, at suburban area of Taipei City, and our Filmmaking Department is on the edge of TNUA's campus, I suggested Lawyer Huang to meet me at Taipei Metro's Guandu station for pickup.

When I was wandering at the front gate of the station looking for traces of Lawyer Huang during my lengthy waiting, I was approached and asked if I was Professor Lee by a mature-age woman dressed in elevated outfits with fashionable appeal. It immediately struck me that she was Lawyer Huang Shiu Lan, who gave me a completely different image compared to my perception of a traditional attorney. Without hesitation, I let her get into my car for the coming speech.

In an easy-to-understand and well thought-out way, Lawyer Huang talked in-depth about different aspects of intellectual property, which was of great beneficial to and guided our students. Thus, inviting Lawyer Huang to teach "IP Rights and Contract Negotiation" course in our MFA Program in Filmmaking for the second semester in AY 2017-18 was an easy decision for me to make. And since then, her class has become the most popular course amongst the students in TNUA's Filmmaking Department.

Lawyer Huang indeed remains in her lawyer character while teaching. Every week her class is well prepared and presented,

and she elaborates on various cases with details so that students can acquire wide range of knowledge in great depth regarding IP rights and contract negotiation in the filmmaking industry.

On top of that, Lawyer Huang's generous sharing of every class's well-prepared content on her Facebook page greatly benefits those in the filmmaking industry and beyond, who subsequently learn more about IP rights and contractual matters.

We can again recognize Lawyer Huang's selfless contribution of her professional knowledge to society when we read this E-book. The story is about EMI Records' use of Taiwan's Amis folksong, "Elder Drinking Song", sung by Mr. and Mrs. Duana (Kuo Ying Nan and Kuo Hsiu Chu), and such use triggered an international infringement lawsuit.

Her story astounded me no less than a detective novel does. I was impressed by how Lawyer Huang handled this claim spanning over a decade. What she experienced throughout the case is similar to that of a detective who tends to search for all the possible leads, collect complete evidence and clarify the development process in order to find out the truth. And yet, Lawyer Huang's reach was beyond a detective's task because she had to devise strategies to prove the defendants' wrongdoing or to have them surrender.

Adapting stories based on professionals' real lives is currently very popular with the production of film and television dramas. I believe the international litigation led

by "Elderly Drinking Song" will also be a good fit for a film adaptation of an IP lawyer's true story.

I would like to present this article as a forward for Lawyer Huang Shiu Lan's E-book and a remembrance of our friendship of five years. In opening this book, readers are on the precipice of recognizing how challenging and how important it is to protect the right of intellectual property.

Forward
Rethinking the Relationship between Culture and Law

Film Director
Ya-Li Huang

Many of my thoughts emerged when I read through the process where Magic Stone Music and Lawyer Huang Shiu Lan were fighting over this copyright infringement case for Mr. Duana(Kuo Ying Nan), who comes from Taiwan's Malan Tribe. My heart is full of admiration for their strong will in dealing with all legal argument challenges and sustaining patience in the lengthy legal proceedings. Reflecting on the complexity between contemporary Indigenous culture and intellectual property, this international IP infringement case that occurred almost 30 years ago stands as an important contribution.

In this case, what draws our attention during the litigation process is that almost 30 years ago, Taiwan's copyright protection was not full-scale legislation; frankly, it felt oversimplified. With the general public's bias and misunderstanding toward the artists' ownership and interests,

the government and society's cognition of creation values like arts and performance was pretty limited.

However, even though we could conclude that the general public lacked copyright awareness when the incident occurred in 1996, we do not see much progress in today's circumstances. Facing the complexity between copyright and art creation, most people are still befriending uncertainty and hesitating to resolve the disputes. There is even no denying that the authority and the entire society have long held indifference toward Indigenous interests and put systemic suppression against Aboriginal people. Therefore, it is not surprising to learn how challenging Mr. Duana's case was in Taiwan at the very beginning.

A key issue is pointed out in Mr. Duana's case: Is there comprehensive protection under Taiwan's law for the copyright of music arrangement or performance in this case? This point was also used by the international defendants' attorneys to feed their argument of Taiwanese legislative omissions that Taiwan's law did not provide an effective safeguard on the claimed rights. Luckily, the act was gradually amended in 1964, 1985, 1990, 1992 and 1993 to cover the insufficiency in each phase and there was still basic reasoning available for Mr. Duana to interpret the law at that time, which enabled the standpoint against those international attorneys and allowed the claims more admissible.

Compared to the right of performance, the underlying

copyright awareness within "music arrangement" spots a particular phenomenon in tribal culture. With the difference in culture and customs, Taiwan's minor ethnic groups often come up with arguments concerning the interpretation of their music: Is singing an old folk song which has been orally passed down for ages considered a "creation"? If the answer is yes, when such a creation had been creatively adapted or recreated, based on what ground and condition the international law could provide such "right of adaptation" (or "right of arrangement") in 1996?

The case ended up that the entitlement of music arrangement copyright could be established because the comparison indicated an over 80% difference between the decades-ago old song and Mr. Duana's 1994 version. Having said that, we have one intriguing question presented here: Provided that we must follow this required scientific method, how can 75% or below 70% difference would be considered insufficient to justify the recognition of song creation? Especially when it comes to the sense of music, using a scientific method to define the slight difference is very arguable. Nevertheless, the outcome indicates the law is somehow the last safeguard for art creation. Considering what it takes to guard the author's dignity, we cannot deny involving scientific measurements to meet a legal standard in order for valid protection, even though the nature of such measures is against the structure and spirit of the music.

It heavily depends on the litigants' reasoning and strategic power to meet the legal requirements, and there is no doubt the process would take both parties' great efforts and resources with full rigor. Needless to say, meeting such legal requirements is likely to create a parallel universe for individuals with poor economic conditions, where they have no entrance ticket to the expensive legal warfare.

Had not Lawyer Huang overcome all kinds of challenges with absolute dedication, Mr. and Ms. Duana given all the trust and consistency, and multinational counsellors demonstrated excellent cross-border work, winning this case would have been impossible. This case has not only become a push to better Taiwan's legislation on copyright laws, but also led to reasonable, legitimate, and rightful respect on the world stage for Taiwan's Indigenous tribal culture.

While various Indigenous rights and social movements were growing by the late 1990, we can see Indigenous copyright legislation containing advanced perspectives has been introduced, and a stronger tie between the culture reviving and political resources has formed in the current decade. These changes have gradually influenced ethical symbols, pattern, music, dance and their orality traditions; moreover, they provoke arguable discussion and debate in the applications and interpretations of numerous cultural images.

The current topics may drive more focus and divert further,

which probably means the party who engaged or was involved is facing and choosing different cultural practices. As the diversity of copyright or proprietary property increases (ex: Protection Act for the traditional intellectual creations of indigenous peoples) throughout all kinds of actions in the future, our comprehension of those topics may also increase.

We know that the concept of copyright originates from the Western legal system; therefore, we are required to find a more flexible measure or develop more negotiation and discussion approach for striking a balance between the tribal culture consisting of collective consciousness and modern law emphasizing individual creation value.

Being the live practice for tribal culture to speak to the public, Mr. Duana's international infringement case has undeniable significance for the time being. The case details, grounds and assertion of legal rights all provide an influential reference to ponder the relationship between creation and legal framework nowadays.

As traditional preservation and modern theory are injected into the legal regulation dividing the ethical groups and the tribal self-awareness thriving between legalization and politicization, the past is inherited, and new ideas are interpreted, a challenge awaits us: How can we be freed from the existing framework, and retain our understanding and respect in the aspect of creation? How can we keep the

openness existing in the cultural flow, and break the barrier encountered while pursuing personal independence? These questions matter to every ethical group or tribe when trying to revive their traditional culture, and yet, trying to answer these questions will lead a march to increase maturation of legislation on copyright and traditional cultural creations.

(July 28, 2022)

Forward
What Follows the War of Honor

The director of Wild Fire Music, Taiwan
Xiong Ru Xian

Deep down I am so grateful that Lawyer Huang has put in writing all the details of this international copyright litigation over the Olympics theme music "Elder Drinking Song" in 1996. This is much more than one copyright claim. This fight is over the cultural justice of music origin. And Huang Shiu Lan is the only person who has experienced all through the legal war.

Having been working in the Chinese music industry for a long time, from the mainstream label group to the independent music brand, I turned away from the profitable dominant market because of Taiwan's Indigenous voice. I was still deeply rooted in the mainstream commercial system at that time when the beautiful voice was calling for me, and the calling was literally taking me off the virtual stage to an in-person space. I remember being so amazed by the Amis elders' singing by Kuo Ying Nan, Kuo Hsiu Chu (Mr. and Mrs. Duana) and the Malan

choir for the first time I heard them. They were swinging and swaying their bodies with steps counting beats, and the song arrangement was so harmonious that no instrument was needed. Because the hundreds-year-old heritage has been passed down by oral tradition, Amis people can compose the song as they want by chanting. The unique polyphony consisting of two or more simultaneous voices presents different layers of melodic lines. The way leading voice and answering voice call each other in a specific lyric form of "functioning word" is no less communicative than any spoken language in the world. And this is the uniqueness of indigenous culture, and its holiness is beyond civilization.

Personally, I called Kuo Ying Nan and Kuo Hsiu Chu "Grandpa" and "Grandma." From the aspect of music, they showed me the world of music; and from the aspect of emotion, they were like my family without a blood tie. In October 1999, I accompanied the couple and the other elders as members of the Malan choir to the "Love & Dream World Music Festival" in Tokyo. Upon our arrival at Hikarie Hall, where the performance was going to take place, the organizer tried to persuade us to cooperate with a famous performer for improvisation. Considering such performance would be lacking a rehearsal, I politely refused. To my surprise, Grandpa Kuo Ying Nan said yes - he was willing to participate in this experiment with "Elders Drinking Song."

Fully interpreting the spirit of Amis folk song, the Malan Choir's performance that day was spectacular. One moment the audience was filled with excitement, and the next moment the audience experienced a gentle wave of calm. At the end of the program, the host invited the improvising performer and the Malan Choir on the stage for the encore song, "Elder Dinking song", in the form of collective improvisation, which gave us a nervous feeling in the pit of our stomach at the backstage. Listening to them at the side bay offstage area, I started feeling discouraged by this unrecognizable performance and distressed by their discoordination. When the music was over, in contrast to the audience's reaction- loud, long, and even standing applause, my stomach sank with pity, because this song was performed in a way that lost its real touch.

While Grandpa and Grandma were stepping off the stage, Kuo Ying Nan was walking ahead, murmuring something in Amis language.

I asked Kuo Ying Nan's son. "What did Grandpa just say?"

The son replied. "Grandpa said, the original song and its improvising version on the stage are like a chicken and a duck."

I could not really get how Grandpa took it so lightly that his song was changed to something else than expected. Nevertheless, as everyone returned to the hotel resting, nothing was mentioned anymore.

Still, I tried to figure out this "chicken and duck" metaphor

for years afterward.

When Kuo Ying Nan heard his own voice on TV played in the Olympics promotional song in 1996, what he faced was not only the infringement on the use of his voice and his works but also ignorant users' disrespectful exploitation of his musical culture consisting of respect and courtesy. The outcome of justice, fairness and respect would not have been achieved without Rock Records and Lawyer Huang's persistence on the legal war against power and arrogance. I will never forget what I saw at the out-of-court settlement press conference (for the copyright infringement over "Elders Drinking Song") held in December 1999, where Grandpa and his wife handed in hands and hugged each other with tears in their eyes for the acknowledgement of this outcome.

Upon receipt of the news that Grandpa Kuo Ying Nan passed away on March 29, 2002, I decided to honor the memory of Grandpa by singing for him. The ceremonial farewell concert, namely "The Note Missed In the Chords," was held in the traditional territory of the Amis in Taitung (now it's Taitung Seashore Park) on April 12. The invitation was sent to Taiwanese musicians of different ethnicities, and every singer took pride in the attendance, regardless of whether he or she personally knew Kuo Ying Nan or not. The following day of the concert was the official funeral, and that was the time to say goodbye to our Grandpa. That day after the funeral, I was

dozing off on the train back to Taipei at noon, and suddenly it struck me that I might have the answer to that lingering question – why would Kuo Ying Nan agree to participate in the performance with that Japanese improvising musician? From Grandpa's point of view, when I am willing to sing and I want to sing for you, I don't mind using the way you would like to have me sing for you. Nothing is holding him back from singing, and there is no concern in his mind because there is no framework for natural expression. Grandpa had no rule for it, and the same for his song. Indigenous folk songs always bring humans back the nature.

While the evolution of civilization requires cultural power to push through, at the same time, the author's ownership and rights should not be violated. Although this lawsuit has drawn global attention to it, without Lawyer Huang's authentic narratives, the facts would never come to light, and we will never know the fact that the "Elders Drinking song" originated from the Malan Tribe of Taiwan's Amis and chanted by the Tribe member, Kuo Ying Nan.

After this holy war, Taiwanese Indigenous youth commenced their movement in the wake of their music. Young people began to take pride in chanting their mother language, passing along their cultural heritage, and reviving the folk song's creation. This event also impressed upon the popular music industry the importance of paying respect to Indigenous music, rethinking

the commercial world's understanding of the rights of cultural musical heritage, and treating each contributing element composing the music with fair and reasonable permission legally and carefully.

PS: The "Malan Choir" is a singing group consisting of six Amis members: Kuo Ying Nan, Kuo Hsiu Chu, Kuo Shiu Ying, Kuo Guo Zhi, Kuo Lin Gu, and Yang Shun Ying. The members made their living by farming.

Preface
Elders Drinking Song-Everlasting Melody Is Never Gone

While reviewing the international litigation proceeding for "Elders Drinking Song", which was taking place more than twenty years ago, I can still remember this case like it was happening yesterday.

In 1996, while the Atlanta Olympics' promotion song was ringing in everyone's ear, an East-West cultural warfare - a tension between Indigenous People and modern record labels, and a confrontation between Amis folk song and western popular music - began, which brought shame on the Olympics and made its tune go off-key. A lawsuit arose, and the final justice had waited long to come after a tangle of years of litigation.

Elders Drinking Song has been passed among Amis People in Taitung for a long time, but it was not known to most people until it was launched as the promotion song for Olympics in Atlanta in 1996. While the sonorous music was presented on the highest global sports stage, having the world appreciate the fullness and pride of the sound, yet, people remained unaware that it was oriented from the valley in Taitung, Taiwan.

In the summer of 1996, it was with mixed feelings that Mr.

Difang Duana (Kuo Ying Nan), an Aboriginal singer from the Amis tribe, heard his voice was used by the German band Enigma without his permission. The positive side is that the world stage's spotlight descended on the tribe's heritage, which made him so proud. The negative side is that this disrespectful behavior violated his right, which worried and offended him at the same time. In the beginning, facing the infringer's aggression, arrogance and rude attitude, Mr. Difang Duana was not expecting justice with his poor resource; luckily, Rock Records and Magic Stone Music were determined to support their singer's right and interests at full power.

Mr. and Ms. Duana had never stepped a foot into the court before, but they decided to file this lawsuit in federal district courts in California. With the trial judge's strong push and both parties' lengthy negotiation, a settlement was reached after three years of suffering. This led to the enactment of Taiwan's Protection Act for the traditional intellectual creations of indigenous peoples and prompted the amendment of the Copyright Act, which additionally provides protection for performances. Also, Mr. Duana's international infringement case has become a leading precedent in intellectual property law, acknowledged by law schools and the music industry.

Nevertheless, very little information about this case is available in Europe and the US, where this infringement occurred. Outside Taiwan, there appear to be some

misunderstanding narratives spread and even untruthful records where the lies carry more weight than the fact! As the lawyer mainly in charge of the litigation, I feel my responsibility and urge to clarify this case. Particularly, this has to be told in a common language so everyone can read the whole story and figure out how the rights were violated. I also need to address the importance of respecting Indigenous songs and culture, and I hope the beautiful music brings true harmony and happiness to the world.

The grand and sonorous voice echoed in valleys, and also resounded across the Olympic stage. But who would have thought, there was greed and disrespect behind the song?

Pushed to the corner, Taiwanese Indigenous singers were left with no choice but to commence legal action against a US record company. In a tangle of years of international litigation, a settlement was finally achieved in Amis people's manner of peace-loving nature. As the court battle was put to an end, it was time for the music to regain its beauty.

I

Disclose the Hidden Voice from East Coast Taiwan

When the Indigenous music echoed in Taitung East Rift Valley and the song flew from mountains to the sea, little did the elderly couple singing "Elders Drinking Song" could imagine, this Amis* song, which has been passed down for centuries, would be presented at the Olympic Games! Not to mention to give rise to a cross-border copyright infringement lawsuit lasting three years long.

Before I get the phone call from Landy**, the promotional video of Olympics Special Report has been showing in front of me on the evening news of China Television Company (CTV) for three days, and I have no idea how many times I've heard this Olympics promotional song already. I only find this sonorous voice a perfect match for the feature of the Olympic Games resembling peace, competition, tolerance, and

*Note: The Amis are an Indigenous Austronesian ethnic group in Taiwan.
**Note: Landy, named in Chinese as Pei-jen Chang, used to be the president of Magic Stone Music (1992-2002), a subsidiary of Rock Records Group.

brilliance. It never crossed my mind that it would be oriented from Taiwan's Amis folksong.

While Landy is about to disclose this breaking news in his usual manner, calmy and with a low-pitch sound, I could still sense some tension in the tone that puts people under pressure. "Lawyer Huang, do you remember Mr. and Mrs. Duana, the Indigenous artists who signed the contract last month? Something happened ..." He pauses.

Of course I remember them, how can I forget? The couple are the oldest artists that Magic Music has ever signed a contract with. When Mr. Difang Duana put his signature on the agent contract, he was already 73 years old!

At first, Rock Records Group had some concerns over the risks and the investment feasibility. But Landy never gave up on his master plan promoting the Indigenous music and combing the folksongs into a collection named "Het Eyland Formosa." Landy's persistence eventually convinced Rock Records Head, so an idealistic rather than realistic decision was made to fulfill this music lovers' dream.

Yet, there was still something to overcome. The artist couple not only have had high respect from the tribe, but also been found the best singers among Amis people. It was not that easy to get them on board. It took Rock Records a lot of effort and time to knock on the tribe's door and show its sincerity to the couple and their family. Finally, the couple came to an

agreement, accepted the offer and signed the first artist agent contract in their life.

So this contract is still fresh from the oven, what can go wrong? A contract dispute? I don't think so.

I just finalized the contract with in-house legal a few months ago, and the contract underwent several discussions and revisions between us. I don't think the contract can go wrong as soon as it leaves the table.

Being a lawyer requires a strong heart. A lawyer has to be prepared for any unexpected and extraordinary disputes. Although contract reviewing does not require an immediate response like in the courtroom, you still can see if this is a capable lawyer once the contract is executed. If the contract terms, conditions or wordings are illogical or ambiguous, problems will arise in the execution, which triggers more significant disputes. So basically, you can tell a good or bad contract drafting by the outcome of the contract execution. Unavoidably, I start to doubt if I overlooked anything in the contract...

Why My Voice on TV?

It turns out it has nothing to do with the artist agent contract; it is something much more unbelievable.

"Lawyer Huang, have you watched the special report about

the Olympic Games on CTV? The background music seems the song sung by Difang Duana. At this moment, we are trying to get more details to confirm it." Says Landy.

"Yes!" I reply, "I've been watching the special report in the past evenings with Shen Chun-Hwa as the anchor. Are you talking about the song they play in the Olympic athletes' clips?" I try to recall. "Is that Amis music? I can't really tell. I just feel it's so sonorous, powerful, and so beautiful! How did you learn that it is their voice? Did you get this information from the Amis artist or their tribe?"

While recalling the footage on CTV evening news around 19:25 last night, I find it hard to believe that the Olympics is using a Taiwanese Indigenous song in their promotional music. How come?

"Difang Duana just called me from Taitung and said that two days ago other tribe members heard the Olympics music on the radio and immediately recognized it was his voice in the background. Then they hurried to tell Duana about this." Landy said. "Watching CTV's special report with the family, Duana and his family confirmed it is his voice, and he said he feels confused and offended - Why does the Olympics use his voice without telling him?"

"They contacted a Taitung councilor for help. After knowing what was going on, the councilor suggested that engaging an attorney is a better way to handle a legal matter like this as it looks like a copyright infringement, which is out of reach for a role of legislator."

Landy continues. "Mr.Difang Duana doesn't know any lawyer. But he remembers he has a contract with us and that is why he called. The staff in our Music Production Department just informed me of this incident, and I reported to Sam*. And Sam would like me to get the answer from you. So, Lawyer Huang, is this a music copyright infringement? What should we do?" By now, Landy finally gets me a clear overview and background explanation.

Whose Voice is This ?

So now it's my turn. First thing first, I need to remind them of holding the facts tight and get experts to testify the evidence.

"Before we can determine if the Olympics promotional song has committed copyrighting infringement, we need to verify if the voice in the song is Difang Duana's. Do you have the Olympics promotional video and Difang Duana's recording or CD? You must run audio forensics with precision equipment to ensure that the voice in both clips comes from the same person

*Note: Sam, named in Chinese as Tuan Chung-Tan, is the Head of Rock Records Group and the president of Rock Records.

before jumping into any conclusion."

Then I shot the other question. "It seems odd to me that there was not any recording made by your company for Difang Duana yet, so how did the Olympics obtain Difang Duana's recording for the song? Did he make that recording before signing a contract with your company?"

"Right now, we have no idea how they got Difang Duana's work. According to his family, the song the Olympics used is called "Elders Drinking Song," which is sung by Amis every year during the harvest festival. Maybe someone taped it during live performance or specifically invited Mr. and Mrs. Duana to sing. Nothing is certain for now. Things just came out, and information we have is very sketchy."

Nevertheless, armed with rich crisis management experience, Landy knows how to speed things up, so he continues. "I already had my staff record the background music of CTV's Olympics Special Report and also asked Difang Duana's family to send us his previous recordings from Taitung so we can run audio forensics. The tapes should arrive this afternoon. Lawyer Huang, are you available this evening? Can you be present with us during the process of voice identification? Then, we can go from there for our discussion on handling the current situation."

"Alright, I'll be there at 4:00 p.m." After this phone conversation, I urge my assistant to gather information about the Olympics promotional video. And the task for me is to review

the applicable laws regarding music and audio work, especially if there are some special regulations governing Indigenous music. Not long, it strikes me since this infringement occurred in the US, I should be searching for the Copyright Law of the United States. Suppose we have this copyright infringement case, then the question to ask is - Who are the victims? What right is infringed?"

The clock is ticking. Before a legal framework can be built up in my head, I need to hustle up to the meeting at Magic Stone Music.

When I set my foot into the office, I see Landy listening attentively with a professional headphone in front of a large stereo behind his desk. As he turns around and notices me, he at once unplugs the headphone and plays the music through the speakers for me. "Lawyer Huang, come to listen to it," Landy explains. "The is Difang Duana's voice in the song, "Return to Innocence" of Enigma's album, "The Cross of Changes."

You can feel the music flows in a very natural and smooth way. The Indigenous song "Elders Drinking Song" begins following the Intro, seamlessly mixed with the English part. Total 4 minates 15 seconds long. Then Landy plays the Olympics promotional song. The music itself of both pieces is identical, except that the promotional song is shorter. Finally, Landy plays both songs synchronously, and they overlap each

other perfectly. You cannot tell one from the other. Based on his expertise in the judgment of music performance, he can conclude that they are the same song.

Is This A Case of Infringement?

Landy's long-awaited question pops out as soon as the music goes off, "Has the Atlanta Olympics committed copyright infringement?" This is also the doubt from the bottom of Mr. and Mrs. Duana's hearts.

"Their use of Indigenous music and song without Indigenous people's permission would constitute copyright infringement." I draw up my conclusion.

Landy leads me to move through and arrive another building where the office of Rock Records is located. In the executive suite, Landy tells Sam about his evaluation and my opinion, this Rock Records Head (nicknamed Sanmao in the music circle) simply raises the same question as Landy did, "Does the Olympics promotional song commit copyright infringement?"

I nod. Then that's it. Sam utters a sentence to initiate this world-famous international music infringement lawsuit, "Let's do it then! It's time to take the legal action!"

Sam asks me how much time I need to prepare my preliminary legal opinion and formulate a plan to move forward. I say it would take around four hours. Then he instructs Landy. "Landy, please arrange a meeting at tonight

10:00 p.m. and have the Production Department, Planning and Publicity Department, and the Artists and Repertoire manager for Difang Duana attend it.First we will let our lawyer assess the situation, give us her analysis of the case and the advice, and then we can table the strategy and steps to handle this matter properly."

Landy nods in agreement and returns to his office to have his secretary make all the contacts. As for me, I have to throw myself into the work for legal opinions right away.

II
Here Comes Copyright Law Protection

It is a tough afternoon. Within a very tight deadline of 4 hours before the late night emergency meeting, I have to come up with advices for the case, which involved bands, music production companies and record labels from different countries. Facts of the case have a long span of 30 years (1966–1996) and occurred across three continents (Asia, Europe, and the North America).

Information about the fact? Very few. Governing laws and applicable jurisdiction? Many.

At least we need to consider the copyright laws in five countries, including Taiwan, the US, France, the UK, and Germany. If you narrow down the targets to Taiwan's Copyright Act, between 1966 and 1996, our country's legislative organization had already amended it up to six times.

After quick research for the amendment history of the Taiwan's Copyright Act, I am slightly relieved. Because I learned our law has been covering the work of lyrics, music, and recording in each version of the Copyright Act. No matter

during which period, this song has been under law protection all the way.

These findings really take some load off my mind. Once this song is confirmed to be protected under the law, our legal action will be taken on a firm step.

However, what comes next is even more challenging.

What categories of works does "Elders Drinking Song" fall into? The ''Lyrics'' and ''Melody''—musical works? Or his voice—the works of performance arts or works of sound recordings? It seems that neither the lyrics was penned nor the music is composed by Difang Duana since this song was passed down by elders in the tribe. The recording was not made by Difang Duan, either. So, there is no ground for Difang Duana to claim that he is the copyright owner of musical works or sound recordings for the song.

Ok, then what about the copyright of arrangement or performance for the song? It was said that Difang Duana had rearranged the melody of "Elders Drinking Song." Landy just confirmed that it is Mr. and Mrs. Duana's voice that appears in the song used by the Olympics.

What's left to be discussed is whether works of performing are protected under Taiwan's Copyright Act?

I hop to look up Taiwan's Copyright Act of 1966 and 1978,

and nothing about "works of the performing" is mentioned in those versions. Wait, aren't the singer's works of performing protected under the copyright? This question sounds shocking to me.

In the next half an hour, I have immersed myself in the legislative process. It becomes clear to me that back that time, the legislators regarded "works of the performance" falling within the categories of "Dramatic and choreographic works" and found it unnecessary to stipulate an independent category titled "works of performance."

However, is "the performance of singing" included in "Dramatic and choreographic works?" It seems the legislators did not take considerable measures for this clarification. Standing on a tight deadline in this case, I'd better go with the flow to assert that Difang Duana owns the copyright to his "works of performance arts" by interpreting "Dramatic and choreographic works" under the Copyright Act. As for the musical works of copyright of the song's arrangement, we have to check with Duana himself later.

Our Kickoff Meeting in a Late Night

Spending the entire afternoon at this case, I managed to put together the summaries of applicable laws, arrange the pieces of the limited information by Magic Stone Music in order, and write down some key point notes. By the time I get home, it is

already past 8 pm. I grab something quick to eat, and then I find myself and my files on the road again, straight to the meeting location, where the head of Rock Record, Sam lives close by. At almost 10 pm, all senior managers and Magic Stone Music's GM, Landy, are already there. Given the nature of this case, no one can take it lightly. Within a short while, Sam shows up, signaling the start of the meeting.

As soon as Sam shifts his weight in the chair, he asks. "Is this a case?"

I nod affirmatively. "Alright then, let's kick off the meeting." says Sam to everybody.

Landy starts with how the infringement case came to light, its development over the past few days, Difang Duana's attitude and his tribe's reaction, followed by me elaborating the facts in the infringement and what legal rights to claim. During my legal analysis, almost everyone raises some inquiries and comes up with different strategies, such as a press conference, a filing of an infringement claim, a request for government support or a call to the Olympics to halt the infringing music. Opinions vary.

Sam says nothing, just listens carefully while others speak out freely. Until 1:00 a.m. I am about to leave as I still have my kids to take care of at home. Sam looks at me, "Lawyer Huang, what's your standpoint? How would you suggest us? Before you leave, could you conclude your opinion from the legal aspect?"

"My proposal is," I say, "we need to know if Difang Duana is on the same page with us first. Suppose he is willing to let the company take care of this dispute, then the first thing he needs to do is to sign a power of attorney. With his written approval, the company is entitled to represent him to deal with the infringement case on his behalf. Let's not forget, once this case is brought to the light tomorrow, the media will come under fire, all the different voices will flood in, even the tribe will play a part in it, and we must be mindful that our man maintains peace of mind under the spotlight."

Without hesitation, Sam makes rapid instruction for Landy to contact Difang Duana and engage the Power of Attorney, as the first thing tomorrow.

I continue pointing out, "In my opinion, there are still some issues requiring clarification. Who recorded Difang Diana's singing performance of "Elders Drinking Song" at that time? And how? Was it under any permission or authorization? What was the occasion when they were invited to perform in France in 1988? Do we have any key person on the list or access to the government units for further details? To prevent misinformation, we should not hold a press conference before we get answers to these questions."

Landy cannot agree with me more, so immediately, he has his secretary arrange the visits to the key people in this case tomorrow. As for me, I am taking responsibility for sending

official inquiries to the government agencies.

Before taking off, I decide to emphasize one more thing. "In addition, we should focus on how to make the best approach to the Olympics, who is now still playing the song all day long. I would suggest that we get a US lawyer as soon as possible and send a warning notice stating that we urge the Olympics to stop playing "Elders Drinking Song," apologize to Mr. and Mrs. Duana in public and settle for the infringement claim. Suppose the Olympics is willing to settle in sincere efforts, the best solution will include an invitation for Mr. and Mrs. Duana to perform this song at the closing ceremony of the Olympics on July 19, so the whole world can see."

This exciting idea puts everyone in such high spirits that the atmosphere reaches a climax in the restaurant. Only Sam stays calm enough to confirm the direction of our strategies and the follow-ups. My watch tells me it is 2:00 a.m. when I leave. I am told the next day that the rest did not leave until 4:00 a.m. - just to finish on the assignment and priorities in crisis management.

A Quick Timeline Overview

The next day, as soon as I set my foot into my office, I start sorting out the pieces of information provided by the record company's managers and categorizing them according to their chronological order, events and involving parties. By doing this, the outline of facts gradually comes to light:

1. "Elders Drinking Song" is called "Sakatusa'ku'edaway a radiw" ("The Second Long Song") by Amis people and usually performed during Amis Harvest Festival every year. Difang Duana has been recognized by his tribe as the first chair amongst Amis singers, leading the performance of singing in tribal rituals for many years.

2. In 1966, a professor in Ethnomusicology (let's call him "Professor X" from now on) discovered this song during his fieldwork on folk music. In 1978, Professor X visited Mr. and Mrs. Duana in Taitung and recorded their performance of "Elders Drinking Song."

3. In 1979, Professor X invited Mr. and Mrs. Duana to the studio of First Record Company for the recording of "Elders Drinking Song." Later on, this recording was published on an album "Amis Folk Song / Traditional Folk Songs Chapter 1".

4. In 1988, under the arrangement by Taiwan Council for Cultural Affairs ("TCCA"), X Art Foundation, chaired by Professor X, invited famous Indigenous artists and groups from various Taiwanese tribes to participate in the Pacific Arts Festival in Europe. Mr. and Mrs. Duana and the Malan Choir were also in the group of visiting performers. They toured several European countries and presented Indigenous music and dance.

5. In 1988, during their tour in Paris, the Maison des Cultures du Monde ("MCM") recorded all the live performances on that day including Difang Duana's. Shortly after, MCM planned to publish Difang's recording as well as all other singing on the same day, but MCM found the recording quality of "Elders Drinking Song" too poor. Hence, MCM contacted Professor X for a better recording and soon obtained an audiotape from Professor X.

What remains unclear is whether this audiotape sent from Taiwan was collected during Professor X's fieldwork in 1978, or the studio recording made by First Record Company in 1979. In any case, MCM made and published the CD, and paid a license fee equivalent to F3,000 to X Art Foundation.

6. The record producer Michael Cretu took over the job from German record company, Mambo Musik, to produce an album named "The Cross of Change" for the band "Enigma." During his inspiration hunting process, Mr. Cretu discovered Taiwan Indigenous vocal polyphony CD published by MCM in a small German record shop. It was "Elders Drinking Song" that caught Mr. Cretu's attention and was sampled to his composition for "Return to Innocence", which was included in the album and published on a global scale by UK Virgin Records through EMI Records in 1993.

7. With EMI's authorization, the International Olympic

Committee ("IOC") used "Return to Innocence", which contains the adaptation of "Elders Drinking Song", for the theme song for the Atlanta Olympics in 1996. This license allows for worldwide use for all the Olympics promotional videos.

The Right Person and the Right Questions

Now we get a better picture of the situation. However, we are still unable to verify the background details in this case. Especially the part of music licensing, which is the turning point.

Rock Records, Magic Stone Music, and I have come to an agreement that we should visit the keyperson, Professor X, in person. After all, we cannot tell the whole story without him, not to mention we have to evaluate the case and proceed in legal action. Can we come across the country's border to file this international lawsuit? Can the Indigenous people bring the copyright infringement claim against international record companies? It all depends on how much more we can find out in this case.

In the late-night meeting hosted by Sam, I said I would take up the case, and just like everyone else, we act in coordination under Sam's instructions to get the facts of the case straight. Because of Landy's high efficiency and Rock Records' good

connection, within 12 hours, we already come in contact with the key person - Professor X.

Besides being the chairman of his X Art Foundation, Professor X is also a national policy advisor to the country's President. We doubt if he is willing to meet us, particularly at a sensitive time as we are about to initiate a lawsuit. How much truth can be revealed by him, the person who enjoys the country's highest fame in the music industry, especially in the part where he is personally involved in the music licensing?

Before the visit, we both have full-of-butterflies stomachs. Landy carries his out-of-courtesy gifts and meets up with me in the park near the bus stop. We walk along a couple of curved alleys and eventually find where Professor X lives.

This interview with Professor X has been "rehearsed" between Landy and me. First, who should be in charge of the questions? Not me, not the lawyer - at least not in the first place. Nobody likes to be interrogated by a lawyer. I'd better be on a need-to-act basis and Landy's back-up.

The deal is that Landy does most of the talking. What are the questions? Well, we must know how he was proceeding with his folksong collection, under what condition Indigenous artist's tour in Europe was arranged, how the audiotape was offered, and if any rights were properly licensed during all of the processes.

Ultimately, we enter the house of Professor X. As usual,

Landy plays as an excellent ice breaker with his charming voice. Landy maintains a polite composure explaining what brings us here, and asks Professor X to recall what happened at the time.

Professor X gracefully takes a seat on his elegant chair. He starts with the collection of Indigenous peoples in Taiwan thirty years ago. With eyes sparkling with achievement, he tells us how he was impressed by Mr. and Mrs. Duana and how much effort he made in facilitating various Indigenous groups to tour Switzerland and other big cities in Europe like Paris. The conversation goes so smoothly that we soon forget to be nervous; instead, we indulge in the history of glory with him.

It is getting late. X Professor's wife is trying to get him to take the med and rest. Knowing our mission is still incomplete, I drop Landy a hint to remind him of those questions about licensing recording live performance in Taitung or Paris. But Landy still attentively listens without uttering a word, apparently not getting any hint from me. But somebody must speak up right now, and it seems there is no choice that person must be me.

So I ask, which takes a certain level of courage, as interrupting somebody's glory moment is certainly not the most welcome thing to do.

As soon as my "sensitive" question pops out, there is a sudden change in the atmosphere. Professor X stares at me, his

face locks into a grimace, and his voice is raised. It doesn't take much to sense his annoyance with me.

"You are too young to imagine how difficult Taiwan's international status was in the 1980s. After Taiwan was expelled from the United Nations and ended diplomatic relations with important countries, it was an incredibly difficult challenge to get an opportunity for Taiwanese Indigenous peoples to perform in major European cities! Wherever they went, they received warm welcomes and earned great appreciation from the audience! No one can deny that it was an extremely tough diplomatic mission!"

Professor X continues. "Achieving such a glorious outcome, yet, you are standing here questioning me if I had any authorization? Any license contract? It was honourable enough for us to present our folk music with Maison des Cultures du Monde. What kind of license or agreement did ever I need? Copyright is common sense for those European countries, and there is no way they would commit infringement. Your investigation should stop, right here, right now!"

Revealing his attitude regarding this tour as a diplomatic victory, Professor X says. "At that time, I found it a great idea that the Maison des Cultures du Monde would like to produce a CD for Taiwan Indigenous artists. It totally made sense to allow them to retain the CD in their premises as to promote Taiwan Indigenous music. Shortly after, MCM's director informed

me that the quality of live recording on that day wasn't good enough, and he asked if I had other tapes. That's why I sent MCM the recording of Duana's "Elders Drinking Song" published by First Record. A couple of years later, I learned the recording was used in an album by another foreign record company, so I wrote them an inquiry email. Very quickly, MCM sent me the music license fee, and I accepted it on behalf of the foundation."

Professor X responds to me: "You see, it was all legitimate, even including signing a licensing agreement!"

III
Anyone Ever Asked the Performers?

But The KEY question remains UNANSWERED.

Did Mr. and Mrs. Duana ever give permission for the music license?

This is important. If the recorders or the producers never obtained the music license from owners of copyrights on the musical works, the so-called "licensing process" between the art foundation and MCM would still not be legitimate.

The displeased look on Professor's face slows down my questioning. Landy is doing his best to calm him down, and I start to hesitate to throw another question that would definitely offend him. However, the legal proceedings may begin anytime after tonight, then there will be no chance like this very moment to address Professor X with these questions. Thinking I might lose the last chance to find out the truth, it does not take me long to go ahead.

"Did Difang Duana ever agree to the recording of First Record or the Maison des Cultures du Monde?"

Not surprisingly, I hit him with his raw nerve.

He gazes at me with rage growing. "Whatever happened in the past belongs in the past. They had performed, and the show was over. What's there to agree to? Period."

I pluck up my courage again to confront him. "So, when the director of Maison des Cultures du Monde asked you to send them the recording of 'Elders Drinking Song,' did you ask for Mr. and Mrs. Duana's permission?"

Professor X simply stands up, showing us to way out. I stare at him and stand still, waiting for my answer.

He walks to the hallway and opens the door. "The tape recording is the property of X Art Foundation. Why did we need their permission?!" He is spitting an angry answer.

He cannot make it more clear that we are leaving. Landy and I sense the objection and begin walking toward the door. We say our goodbyes, politely.

Landy and I are only in our thirties, in the prime of our youth. We cannot swallow his story, and an ending like that cannot close our curiosities and sense of justice. Walking out of the Professor's house, we take a stroll to the nearby park with full of lingering doubts and uneasiness. Landy cannot hold it anymore. "It looks like they never got authorization from the artists throughout the entire process. How come he still gave an account of himself in such a proud way? What breakthrough in diplomatic difficulties, the nation's glory... Total hypocrisy for him to lecture us like that! Lawyer Huang, what are you

suggesting?"

"Frankly, it would not be fair to let Professor X take all the blames. It must have been so challenging to group the Indigenous peoples on the international stage considering Taiwan's poor international status and rigid political situation at that time."

I continue my thoughts. "All levels of society had very little awareness of copyright protection at that time. I believe Professor X was not the only one who thought that way. Back then, it was common for people with high academic titles or high ranks to use splendid excuses like national glory so they could justify what they did to chase their personal reputation by sacrificing other individuals' interests. Take one step back, considering his role and position are so critical in this case, it's not wise to be on the other side with Professor X. Frankly speaking, it will be so much of help if he can stand up for Difang Duana and be in our favor against the foreign infringers."

Staring at the gloomy streetlights in the park and the full moon in the sky, I finish what I need to say. Landy nods and accepts the reality in silence. And it is time to go home.

A Late and Unjustifiable Offer

Once I get home, I bury myself with the materials of copyright laws in different countries again as there are still

many questions requiring clear answers.

Who are the infringers? Which Act was, has been, or is being violated? And in which year did the violation happen?

I need to confirm the answer, organize the information and pass it to Magic Stone Music, and then they will turn it over to Dewey Ballantine LLP in Los Angeles, who has been retained by Mr. and Mrs. Duana. This research work will help this US law firm draft the official demand letter on a solid factual and legal footing.

While the demand letter is being drafted in the US, our ongoing investigation is still underway. Like searching for pieces for a jigsaw puzzle, we are making our best effort in an attempt to consult the relevant parties through different channels.

While we track down the friends and relatives of Difang Duana and have them recall what happened in 1978 regarding the recording, I also write to Taiwan's Council for Cultural Affairs ("TCCA") and X Art Foundation requesting the records and documents related to Mr. and Mrs. Duana's performance in France in 1988.

My attorney letter was sent to X Art Foundation on July 5, 1996, and later in their response, they claim that they do not retain any relevant documents because they were not the organizer at that time. Nevertheless, they admit having received half of the license fee of ₣15,000 from the Maison des Cultures

du Monde regarding Enigma's production of the album, "The Cross of Changes", and now X Art Foundation is willing to share this amount equally with Mr. and Mrs. Duana.

Through his family, Difang Duan asks our record company and me if they can accept the offer. I explain to them that it is unwise to take it. Because at this very moment we are about to start the legal proceedings, if Mr.Duana accepts the offer and the money will be considered the price for granting the license, then what cause of action or right does he have to bring the lawsuit for infringement?

I make Difang Duana and his family think, can they accept "taking the money" - no matter the amount is whole or half of F15,000 - as an answer to everything that has happened so far?

A few days later, they have come to understand what is missing in this picture. The world misses the truth. People will never know the song "Elders Drinking Song" comes from Taiwan, if we do nothing. Difang Duana and his family find unacceptable to end this dispute; instead, things should be taken care of in other way. So they decide to refuse the offer of the late licensing fee.

Lost in Translation, or Lack of Awareness?

On the other hand, 20 days later the Taiwan Council for Cultural Affairs ("TCCA") response arrives, expressing that no relevant records or information are documented in their files.

I am not exactly expecting such a short answer from them, honestly, I am quite disappointed.

According to Professor X, the international situation was so difficult for Taiwan at that time; when such a vast opportunity arose for TCCA to lead the Indigenous performers to visit Europe, it is odd to me that nothing was put down in black and white for this official international event.

As a lawyer, I don't surrender easily, especially when collecting the evidence for my case. Finally, I track down one of the key persons, Mr. Hsu Shao-jen, who accompanied the tour to France in 1988. He is kind enough to describe some part of the facts that he can remember.

Over the phone, he recalls. "It was Mr. Hsu Ying-zhou who had a contract with TCCA to organize the overseas visiting tour. However, the said contract is lost. And there was also an agreement between TCCA and the Maison des Cultures du Monde ("MCM"). When MCM requested to record the live performance by Difang Duana and others, Hsu Ying-zhou expressed his disagreement, but no one else from TCCA said anything. As for the agreement between Professor X and MCM over the live recording? I have no idea."

Neither Magic Stone Music nor I can be certain that what he says is the actual fact of the case. All we can tell is we need a further check. Three days later, we have a chance to interview Mr. Huang Wu-chung, an inspector of the TCCA's Performing

Arts Section, who accompanied the tour and was in charge of the expenses and administrative work during the trip in 1988.

According to Mr. Huang, TCCA did not sign any contract with the Maison des Cultures du Monde that year. However, the fax communications between them included a consent letter. And the agreement between TCCA and Mr. Hsu Ying-zhou existed. When the MCM started recording like they usually would do to the performers on the stage, TCCA staff was not capable to speak up or make objection due to incompetence in the French language.

What Mr.Duana Says

It appears none of the officials can provide us with any documents stating what happened in France that year. It becomes almost impossible to prove whether TCCA had a written agreement with the Maison des Cultures du Monde to allow the live recording. Even there were written consent from TCCA, it could be invalid, because the licensing does not hold up without the actual performer's consent in the first place.

So, in the end, we still need to come down to Mr. and Mrs. Duana's confirmation of whether they ever gave permission to anyone or charged the license fee for recording their performances, which include:

1966, the collection of Indigenous music by Professor X at his fieldwork; 1978, live recording by Professor X in

Taitung; 1979, studio recording at First Record; and 1988, live performance recording in France.

Even at the age of 74, Mr. Difang Duana still has a good memory comparing with young people. Just like flipping a page in his diary, it doesn't take too much effort for him to recall what happened.

"In 1978, Professor X came to Taitung and asked us if we could sing to him. He said he would like to record us. The following year, we were invited to Taipei for recording, and we did not receive anything either. Money...? No, he brought us a bottle of millet wine as a gift."

He continues. "The trip to France? Well, I was simply told to sing on the stage. The recording was not even on my radar. Actually, my wife was feeling sick that day, so she was just sitting with the audience... No idea what those foreigners were talking about... No clue about who was presenting TCCA as I did not really know anyone. The only face I could recognize was Professor X. With that being said, he did not tell us much about the performance, either."

It seems we have a clearer understanding of what that was all about. Time to draw the conclusion:

Difang Duana never permitted anyone to record his performance in France or license such recording to Maison des Cultures du Monde or EMI Records for adaptation or

publication.

Thus, all the uses of the recording of Duana's "Elders Drinking Song" by the Maison des Cultures du Monde, EMI Records, and the Atlanta Olympics are considered copyright infringements.

A Walk-through of Facts in the Case

While verifying the facts and the details of the infringements, I completed the analysis of the copyright laws of the related countries in the recent 30 years (1966–1996), confirming the copyrights that Difang Duana owns regarding "Elders Drinking Song." At a minimum of law protection, he has copyrights in the musical adaptation and his work of performing for the song.

I can finally walk through the facts of the case in the order in which the events occurred:

1. For Amis People, the Indigenous tribe on the East Coast of Taiwan, "The Second Long Song" carries ancestors' creation across time. In their mother language, it is called "Sakatusa' ku'edaway a radiw," and in English we name it "Elders Drinking Song."

This song was further arranged by Mr. Difang Duana, and used to be sung in harmony with his wife Ms. Igay Duana, particularly in the so-called "counterpoint" way.

In 1978, the ethnomusicologist, Professor X, recorded Mr. and Mrs. Duana's songs during his fieldwork on Taiwan's

folk music. The entire audio recording session of "Elders Drinking Song" was completed at the premises of their relative in Taitung. Following that, Professor X invited Mr. and Mrs. Duana to record "Elders Drinking Song" in First Record Company in Taipei. At that point, Mr. and Mrs. Duana gave Professor X oral consent to use the sound recording for educational purposes only.

Nevertheless, Professor X still used their sound recording by First Record Company for cassette tapes production and put them for sale. In the following year (1979), Professor X released the album on CD and kept this work in his X Art Foundation. Yet, all of this all underwent without notifying Mr. and Mrs. Duana of his use.

2. In May 1988, X Art Foundation was invited by the French Ministry of Culture and Education to lead Taiwanese Indigenous performers to the Maison des Cultures du Monde in Paris ("MCM") for "Pacific Aboriginal Dance and Music Festival." Thanks to the Council for Cultural Affairs sponsorship, Mr. and Mrs. Duana were able to join the team. After the commencement of the performance, MCM recorded the live singing without the prior consent of Difang Duana and the others.

Later, MCM would like to cooperate with X Art Foundation to collect folk music for producing an album and release it on CD to the market. Considering the quality of the live recording

at MCM was not good enough, MCM requested Professor X to provide a clear version of "Elders Drinking Song." Thus, the recording made in First Record Company in 1979 by Professor X was provided to MCM without any written agreement to document this right transfer. Only the Maison des Cultures du Monde and X Art Foundation are mentioned on the CD cover, and there is not any traces or credit given to the performers, Difang Duana and Igay Duana.

3. In 1993, Virgin Record Company of Germany commissioned Mambo Musik Company to produce the album "The Cross of Changes" for the band "Enigma". On April 4 of the same year, Mambo Musik made a payment to MCM. On April 19, MCM and the producer Michael Cretu entered into a licensing agreement which entitled Cretu to use "Elders Drinking Song." So Michael Cretu could sample it to the composition of his contemporary single "Return to Innocence."

In the licensing agreement, MCM warranties having ownership of the master tape, and claims to have obtained all necessary license; in addition, MCM represents that all the rights holders, including MCM and the artists, have transferred all the right they can claim.

As soon as the album "The Cross of Changes" was released, it hit TOP Billboard 100 and stayed as long as 32 weeks. The album also reached the world's top four on this record chart and

remained such a high raking for four weeks, with total sales of over 6 million copies.

In Taiwan, the album was released through EMI Taiwan. In the US, the album was released by Charisma Records who located in New York. Charisma Records obtained the exclusive license from Virgin Schallplatten GmbH for publishing in the US market. The manufacturer of the album's CD is Capitol Records, Inc., a subsidiary of a California-based company named Capitol-EMI Music.

4. In August 1995, the chairman of X Art Foundation sent a Copyright Statement to the MCM. This statement mentioned that the copyrights in any sound recording published by X Art Foundation are owned or deemed to be owned by the performing signers or group because these artists are considered the author or composer of the subject music.

Later on, the chairman tackled the licensing deal negotiation with MCM in August 2005, and MCM's payment of ₣15,000 was remitted to X Art Foundation.

5. In 1996, the Atlanta Summer Olympics used the unique music passage of "Elders Drinking Song" contained in "Return to Innocence" as a television advertisement to promote Olympics. The performing singer, Mr. and Mrs. Duana, were never recognized by any means, and they were never paid by anyone in any form of license fees or royalties.

IV
Time to Speak Up

I have presented the facts in the copyright infringement case to the senior management of Rock Records. As soon as Sam and Landy read these facts, they decided to retain an American counsel for sending the letter of claim to the infringing parties, including EMI Records, the Olympics, and MCM. We include a clear statement that the infringers are obliged to respond in a limited time for the compensation of the infringement; otherwise, our claims will be filed to the court.

Notwithstanding we fire the first shot for the battle of our international copyright protection for "Elders Drinking Song," whether it leads to a war or peace still depends on the responses from the infringers.

Different Voices

The breaking news of Amis music work being infringed upon overwhelms the people on our island. Taiwanese media disclosure is attracting all kinds of concerns and comments from people from different parts of society; some criticize those

foreign record labels and the Olympics; some applaud and feel proud with the rise of Amis music on the international stage.

However, over the issue of whether Mr. and Mrs. Duana are the copyright holders and entitled to bring a lawsuit, most people in the intellectual property industry, authorities and academia tend to believe that singers have no copyright for lyrics and music in the song. A general saying is neither lyrics nor music of "Elders Drinking Song" was written or composed by Difang Duana; instead, it is a song passed down by Amis people through generations. Some disagree that Mr. Duana has copyright protection to his performance due to the lack of relevant regulations in copyright laws. Another strong voice indicates that Mr. Duana has no title to the sound recording in the album as the recording was not made by him...

Differing opinions in those press releases against our position is flooding in, the pressure landed on Rock Records' shoulder can be imagined. Even during a TV interview, one official from the Copyright Committee of the Taiwan Ministry of the Interior stated that Indigenous peoples do not enjoy any rights in "Elders Drinking Song." Such remarks almost crushed our confidence of the fight for Mr. and Mrs. Duana's interests.

Thanks to the long-built trust on the tight cooperation between Rock Record and me over the years, Rock Record has faith in me and my assessment beyond the shadow of a doubt.

This unfriendly situation does not unnerve us. We have our

feet on the ground, preparing for the copyright infringement case with vitality. Within the tightest time frame, Rock Records and I manage to have another milestone meeting, discussing how to formulate and implement the upcoming litigation, media strategies, evidence collection and other essential steps.

Rock Records and I reach a consensus on bringing the case to the legal procedures in the meeting, and we induce a team to get in touch with some of the leading US law firms. To grab the maximum attention, we aim to ring the bell in the Olympics Game duration, and since the major field of battle is set in the US, which naturally leads our first round of legal action to take place in the US.

We have no idea that among ten leading US law firms we consult with, only two respond to us with follow-up interests. The other eight firms imply that they would not want to take our case and offend the powerful and influential opposing parties-EMI Records and the International Olympics Committee.

We even receive a couple of abrupt rejections from the Public Relations agencies because they also prefer not to stand on the opposite side of EMI Records. The only PR agency showing some interest gives us such a high price that we cannot possibly accept. So not voluntarily, the head of Rock Records puts aside this strategy of waging a media war in the US, and decides to save all the focus on the collaboration with US law firms.

Under the Spotlight

There is no way to escape from the domestic media reports. The Taiwanese media during this crisis is creating huge chaos. Some reporters run into the premise of Mr. and Mrs. Duana in Taitung asking for an interview; some newspapers keep speaking out negatively on our action by quoting some scholars or officers' comments. Our records companies are chased to disclose the latest development, even some foreign medias have joined the news war. Magic Stone Music thus decides to hold a press conference on July 2, 1996.

The day before the press conference, Rock Records invited Mr. and Mrs. Duana to Taipei. I bring them the documents for power of attorney in both Chinese and English to sign. While everyone else is busy, Mr. Duana and I happen to have a chance to grab some chat.

The first time talking to a lawyer, he looks slightly nervous and intense, and I am trying to find some way to ease his tense mood. We sit down by the window, looking out and enjoying the glazing Taipei night view. I decide to call him "Grandpa" like everyone else.

"Grandpa, how do you feel about the trip to Taipei? How do you like Taipei?"

Looking out of the window and pondering for a while, Mr. Duana says. "The buildings in Taipei are so small, like

matchboxes..."

Lightheartedly, I say. "Yeah...Taipei, full of high-rises, cars, and people. Grandpa, did you want to go back home to Taitung as soon as you arrived in Taipei?"

He laughs a pure, child-like laugh. "What I really want right now is to sing in the valleys of Taitung." For a moment, he was relaxed, being reminded of his favorite thing in the world, singing.

It's the same night that Magic Stone Music faxes me the drafts of the invitation and press release for the next day's conference. After I make some corrections and finalize the wordings, the Planning and Publicity Department of Magic Stone Music, within the shortest possible time, have the invitation and press release send over to every journalist they know, regardless of printed or electronic media.

Invitation: Press Conference for Difang Duana

This best-selling single "Return to the Innocence" by Enigma, with millions of copies sold worldwide, has recently been used as the theme song of 1996 Summer Olympics. While this song is enjoyed and known by people all over the world, very few are aware that the ethereal voice sampled in "Return to the Innocence" comes from an Indigenous couple in Taitung, Taiwan — Mr. and Mrs. Duana.

In spite of such contribution, Mr. and Mrs. Duana's voice is never recognized in either Enigma's single or the Olympics

theme song. Mr. and Mrs. Duana have never received the fair and respectful treatment they deserve. So far, this affair has caught worldwide attention and been disclosed by national and international media, which starts to make their contribution gradually known to the world.

However, it appears that the parties involved in this matter come from different countries; the details at this moment seem to remain unclear. Mr. Difang Duana finds it is necessary to clear the air and tell the society where he stands. Thus, we are going to hold this press conference to let Mr. Duana speak for himself in person.

In January 1996, a group of six Amis singers, including Mr. and Mrs. Duana, contracted with Magic Stone Music. They authorize Magic Stone Music not only to produce their records but also to represent them on any legal affairs. On the day of official press conference, along with Mr. and Mrs. Duana, Magic Stone Music will announce how the procedures toward the legal solution will be implemented.

Time: Tuesday, 14:00, July 2, 1996
Place: Northsouth Gate, B1, Shangri-La Far Eastern Plaza Hotel, Taipei No. 201, Section 2, Dunhua South Road
Contact: Magic Stone Music

Simultaneously, the Planning and Publicity Department of Magic Stone Music issued a press release. It reads:

"As of today, Magic Stone Music Co., Ltd. officially represents Mr. Difang Duana and Mrs. Igay Duana in handling the copyright infringement case regarding 'Elders Drinking Song' through our Legal Counsel, Huang Shiu-lan. We are now in the process of gathering the evidence. Moreover, Magic Stone Music will not take any benefit shall any monetary compensation be awarded in this claim.

Needless to say, we are proud to see Mr. and Mrs. Duan's performance at 'Elders Drinking Song' appealing to the world and popularized across the Olympics stage. At this moment, Magic Stone Music represents Mr. and Mrs. Duana seeking appropriate attorneys who practice in the infringement location to take up the case.

Should any party be proved to have violated the rights of Mr. Duana, Magic Stone Music will take legal action against the violating parties, regardless of whether they are the government unit, international corporations or International Olympic Committee."

It's the morning of July 2, Landy and I are preparing Mr. and Mrs. Duana for what they only need to say to give their standpoint at the press conference:

"It is Mr. and Mrs. Duana's voice in the promotion song for the Olympics.

This dispute is going for legal process and the lawyers are to handle this international infringement claim.

The most important of all, we are determined to let the whole world know that "Elders Drinking Song" is a song originated from the Amis in Taitung, Taiwan."

Difang Duana gives me a subtle nod, but somehow I can cast the glance of slight discouragement from his clear eye.

"Anything wrong?" I ask. "Grandpa?"

"I've never been to a court in my life, and I never thought I would get into a lawsuit at this age..."

I smile. "Grandpa, don't worry! You only need to say about your position, and we'll take over from there." He gradually regains his composure and remains quiet.

The press conference held on that day went smoothly. With news all over the media coverage, we have received enthusiastic feedback. As this topic is widely discussed, many people attempt to take advantage of the situation and use the opportunity to make a name for themselves along the way. The general opinion is that Difang Duana does not to own any rights to the song. In other words, many people believe what waits for us in this upcoming international infringement litigation is likely to be a defeat, not a victory.

Amongst the outsiders, only the Copyright Committee of the Ministry of the Interior, the competent authority taking charge of copyright affairs, begins to change its attitude and voluntarily provide information. They even have a senior staff check the progress in the case and show the government's supportive

attitude. But what it takes to fight against the international infringers are far more than just polite calls with concerns or some answered inquiries on statutory information.

In short, we are on our own in this case.

In light of the first Indigenous music infringement case in the history of Taiwan, it is pity that our government's hands are so tied that no legal support, manpower, administrative assistance or any other form of resource can be provided to intervene in this infringement case.

Although the majority of Taiwanese people, our government and academic institutions are not optimistic that we have a chance to win, Rock Records and Magic Stone Music do not show any sign to quit. Now we are backed up with Mr. and Mrs. Duana's commitment, there is nothing to stop us from taking further legal action and showing our determination against infringers.

Press Conference Boosted by Taipei City Government

It has been over two weeks that most Taiwanese media are still standing unsupportive to Mr. and Mrs. Duana's attempt to fight for their rights. Unavoidably, Magic Stone Music and I both feel we are fighting alone in a hard battle.

Meanwhile, worn out by endless questions from the journalists, the management of Rock Records, Magic Stone Music and their staff in the Planning and Publicity Department

are looking for new solution to the media mass. It is good timing that the Taipei City government reaches out to us and shows interest in holding a press conference for Mr. and Mrs. Duana as a way for support. Through Landy, Sam learns the news, and the management of Rock Records decides to take the chance. It's July 17 that Taipei City government picks up Mr. and Mrs. Duana from Taitung to attend the international press conference, which will be held on the following day.

The press conference is set to start at 2 PM on July 19, 1996. Landy and I already arrive at the venue by 1 PM, where we stay in the hallway to discuss and confirm the the process and details of the conference. Our plan is that Landy will start the conference by revealing the background of the dispute, and proceed with the introduction of Mr. Difang Duana, Mrs. Igay Duana and the Malan Choir. Then Mr. Duana will talk about his feelings and decisions, followed by Landy's explanation of the issues in the infringement case and the standpoint of Rock Records and Magic Stone Music.

It will be me to announce what legal actions will be taken over this matter. All of this talk will probably take 30 to 40 minutes, and we will leave 10-15 minutes for press inquiries right after. In the end, we will have Mr. and Mrs. Duana and the Malan Choir perform "Elders Drinking Song," so the conference has an ending in the echo of the Indigenous song.

It's not 2 PM yet, the conference venue on B1 of Far Eastern

Plaza Hotel is already packed with reporters and rows of cameras. A busy scene you can envision. Photographers are trying to secure the best position to shoot, and journalists are flipping through the press release published by Magic Stone Music. Some reporters are on the phone arranging the evening broadcast time with TV networks.

"Elders Drinking Song" by Mr. and Mrs. Duan blaring through the venue's speaker warms up the crowd, and the couple's voice also gets everyone's heart to start racing with excitement. Finally, the arrival of Mr. and Mrs. Duana in traditional Amis clothing causes quite a commotion and keeps the cameras flashing nonstop.

With strong curiosity and heated expectation, imagine what a battle the audience is waiting for: The infringed party - An elderly couple of Indigenous singers vs. The infringing party – the Olympics and famous international record companies. The large discrepancy of bargaining power between them is almost uncomparable. No wonder there is eagerness in Taiwanese society to know what the couple will say – about their feelings, their standpoint and their decision.

At the noisy press conference, Landy's deep voice briefing of the details and context surrounding of the case immediately turns the crowd into silence, till there is an explosion of applause from the audience at the introduction of Mr. and Mrs. Duana.

Difang Duana looks shyly, and he stands up to give his remark. He says that he is happy to see the song rise to the international stage; however, it is odd that no one knows that he is the singer. He conveys his decision to seek justice against the Olympics, and with the support of Rock Records and Magic Stone Record, he would like to make it known to the world that "Elders Drinking Song" is a song of Amis people from Taitung, Taiwan.

Skillfully taking over the microphone, Landy gets to the point explaining the issue and the expectations from the musicians as well as Indigenous peoples.

When my turn comes, besides making some supplement to the previous briefing, I speak of our upcoming legal actions against the Olympics and EMI Records. The actions include a formal notice through an attorney's demand letter, demanding them to make immediate correction and apology, admit the act of copyright infringement, restore the artists' names, and compensate for the damages.

When Mr. and Mrs. Duana and the Malan Choir's performance of "Elders Drinking Song" lights up the venue and everyone, the conference vibe reaches to its peak. By the end of song signaling the end of the conference, Landy wraps up the press conference on a perfect note.

First Approach to Infringing Parties

The senior management of Rock Records has been carrying the strong expectation from Mr. and Mrs. Duana and their tribe, also has been aware of their responsibility of protecting their signed artists' interests and Indigenous music. In fact, before the press conference, they already engaged the US law firm, Dewey Ballantine LLP, to draft a demand letter to explain how the Maison des Cultures du Monde and Enigma is found liable for their infringement on Mr. and Mrs. Duana's copyright in the performance of "Elders Drinking Song" and claim the reasonable compensation.

The draft of the demand letter is discussed back and forth until we finally confirm. We have the official demand letters sent out on July 18, 1996. The recipients include EMI Records in UK and Mambo Musik in Germany, with copies to the International Olympic Committee and the Maison des Cultures du Monde.

After receiving our demand letter, on Thursday, July 26 in the US, EMI Records asked Bernard J. Fischbach, the attorney representing Virgin Records, who produced the album for Enigma, to call Kelly C. Crabb, our legal counsel in the US.

Lawyer Fischbach confirms EMI's receipt of the demand letter over the phone. Then our lawyer confronts him by asking how they respond to the fact that the passage of "Elders

Drinking Song" used in Enigma's album is not the recording made in MCM in 1988, instead, the recording was provided by Professor X, and it was released by First Record Company in 1979.

At first, Virgin Records' attorney denied our claim of copyright infringement as they argued that the right in the recording was held by Professor X; hence, the use of the song has nothing to do with Mr. and Mrs. Duana. Which is apparently an attempt to shirk their responsibility.

At the end of the conversation, however, maybe out of curiosity, Virgin Records' attorney still threw a question. "What does Mr. Difang Duana want?" Our attorney forwarded this question to us; namely, we need to prepare for answering the questions: What are the terms for Mr. and Mrs. Duana to settle?

The response from EMI Records to our demand letter of copyright infringement excites the management of Rock Records and Mr. and Mrs. Duana. Among the one-sided discouragement of Taiwanese media, Virgin Records' attorney's approach is undoubtedly a positive reinforcement and shows their concern about this transnational legal action.

Despite of this multinational record label's bold and snobbish attitude toward us over the phone, I can see they are also being careful about this accusation of copyright infringement as this is likely to become international litigation. Particularly the song is licensed to the Atlanta Olympics and it is the first time

in history that a dispute over the copyright infringement of the Olympic promotional music. In the middle of the once-in-four-year Olympic Games, the timing is sensitive.

We can imagine the pressure from the licensee, the International Olympic Committee ("IOC"), is putting on the shoulder of EMI Records. No wonder EMI Records requested the attorney representing Virgin Records to make a call to seek the clarification and ask what this Indigenous couple wants.

V

Can We Achieve Settlement Before Going to Court?

Now, there is a question that needs to be answered by us. To every copyright holder, the first thing they would want is to have their ownership read aloud and clear, which means that the priority for the copyright infringers is to admit in public who the actual copyright owner is.

Therefore, in the meeting over the settlement terms, the first thing Rock Records and I agree upon is to demand EMI Records and the IOC to make a public announcement that the voice behind "Elders Drinking Song" is from Mr. and Mrs. Duana, who come from Amis tribe in Taitung, Taiwan. At the same time, we will also ask EMI Records and the IOC to apologize for using the song without asking for the singer's prior consent.

With the right owner's dignity being secured, we are now looking at how much substantial damage can be claimed for copyright infringement in this case, which involves the loss in the royalties on CD sales and the licensing fees, in addition to

the damages derived from the violation of moral rights.

The damages arising from copyright moral rights infringement are usually not set by laws, so the plaintiff cannot come up with a statutory award with a specific amount under the laws.

Speaking to the decision-makers in Rock Records, I suggest they should consider the economic loss of the copyrighted property, as record companies are more familiar with calculating royalties and licensing fees, and it is easier for Rock Records to get a grasp of the relevant data. But who can be sure about actual statistics on the global sale for these multinational record labels?

"Lawyer Huang, it's true that we are familiar with calculating CD price and percentage of artists royalties. But we have no clue about how much profit EMI Records has made from the sales of the album "The Cross of Changes." And What is the total number of the sales of the album? How much is the licensing fee collected from the IOC for the song "Return to Innocence?" We have no idea. Without accurate numbers on these bases, how can we establish the compensation?" The president of Magic Stone Music asks me this key question in the enthusiastic discussion over the compensation items.

This missing number is truly our bottleneck for damage calculation, so the CFO of the company continued. "Can we

ask EMI Records to provide us with the relevant data or their licensing agreement?"

"I'm afraid that would be difficult. Virgin's attorney shows that they're desperate to get rid of the liability for copyright infringement. How can they voluntarily provide us with the trade secrets and financial revenue of EMI Records? The only legit channel to get the data on these amounts is through a court-mandated investigation. However, the litigation has not yet started, and no such legal investigation or audit can be activated."

While explaining the legal procedures, I take out the fax from the reporter and pass it to the CFO. "Here I got an idea, look, one zealous China Post journalist reported this story and continued with inquiries to EMI's senior management. According to the EMI's response, over five million copies of this album have already been sold worldwide. Maybe we can calculate the singer's royalties based on this figure."

Digesting the information on the faxed paper, the CFO counted the number of tracks in this album. Then he speaks. "If a CD is sold at NT$250 per copy, and there are nine tracks on the CD... First, divide it by 10 tracks for easier calculation and then take 20% as the artist's royalty percentage. The artist can get NT$5 in royalties for each CD sold. We can claim royalties based on the global sale of 5 million copies, in addition to the moral damage and the IOC's licensing fee. Do you find the

calculations for compensation reasonable?" The CFO wants to confirm if this formula can work.

"As far as I know, it is not likely that a singer can get as high as 20% of the CD price for royalties in the US music industry. We need to do double-check for the facts." Against his optimism bias, I do not want to have an overly sunny outlook on the sum of the settlement. Instead - the calculation should be based on actual business practices in the records industry.

"Let's not forget, the other half voice of the song "Return to Innocence" belongs to Enigma, Mr. and Mrs. Duana's part only accounts for one half of the song. That is a 50/50 royalty split." The president of Magic Stone Music, Landy, makes a good point.

Then we have another round to review the album and the royalty items, and we also look into the documents provided by our American counsel, who enlisted the items that artists can claim in the US.

I find myself been sitting in this meeting for over 2...or 3 hours, and this is about time to draw an initial conclusion:

In the song "Return to Innocence" of the album "The Cross of Changes" by Enigma, Mr. and Mrs. Duana's copyrights cover the arrangement and the performance of "Elders Drinking Song". Based on this, the royalty percentage for Mr. and Mrs. Duana should be 1/18 (one eighteenth) as 1/9 (one ninth) of the total number of tracks divided by two equals 1/18. Not

only can the royalty split be applied to this rate, but also the licensing fees. We will have to leave the specific numbers to our American counsel to investigate the actual sales of the album "The Cross of Changes." The compensation calculation also depends on how broadcasting regulations are set out in the US. Meanwhile, we will request a new profit split deals on the royalties for future sales, and our singers' names should be placed in the Album titles.

I pass the meeting conclusions to our American counsel, and he promises that he will work to go through his channels for the album "The Cross of Changes" sales statistics and draft the letter addressing the settlement terms.

It's one week later, Rock Records' management double-checks the draft of the settlement offer letter and lets me pass their confirmation back to our American counsel, who shall fax out the offer to Virgin Records on the following day (August 1).

So what's next? Let's wait and see, with patience.

First Denial

It takes two full weeks to receive the infringing parties' responses from our American counsel.

"The lawyer representing Virgin Records and I had some discussion today (August 14). In their understanding, Mr. and Mrs. Duana's recording of 'Elders Drinking Song' was made in 1966, and the record was published in Taiwan in 1979.

They questioned that Taiwan didn't have an internationally recognized copyright law in 1966, so the recording is not entitled to copyright protection under US law. Therefore, EMI Records does not need to compensate for the damages."

What an outrageous statement, it shows not only they want to shift their responsibilities, but also despise the status of Taiwan's law."

I did not expect what we have been waiting for turns out to be such an irresponsible response. Feeling furious and worried, Rock Records' management and I can start to tell that the negotiation is going to be hard.

On the other hand, we cannot simply ignore the issues challenged by the opposing party. So I give a speedy review on the files and relevant materials, and expound upon the key points to our American counsel.

(I) According to the description of the album "Polyphonies Vocales Des Aborigènes De Taiwan" published in France, Mr. and Mrs. Duana's recording of "Elders Drinking Song" was made in France in 1988, which suggests that the voice sampled in Enigma's album was also made in 1988;

(II) EMI Records should prove that the recording in dispute was made in 1966 if they insist this is the case;

(III)Taiwan enacted the Copyright Act in 1928 and was subject to the reciprocity of copyright protection and

enforcement based on the Sino-American Treaty of Friendship, Commerce and Navigation of 1946. According to Article 4 in the Agreement for the Protection of Copyright signed by Taiwan and the US in 1993, it is stipulated that the Taiwanese copyright holder has the same treatment under US copyright laws, with its protection effective retrospectively as of 1965. Hence, whether Mr. and Mrs. Duana's recording was made in 1966 or 1988, their copyright has always been protected under US copyright laws.

With the collection of the relevant regulations, our American counsel passes these points to Virgin Records's attorney two days later.

It turns out to be another frustrating reply; Virgin Records' attorney comes up with their research pointing out on the phone that the US is not subject to the Agreement for the Protection of Copyright signed by Taiwan and the US in 1993. This argument is ridiculous. This totally doesn't make any sense.

So, on August 23, one day after we received the unreasonable response, we have our American counsel enlist a couple of cases supporting that the Agreement is valid and enforceable in US courts, which means that the Agreement's contents are binding upon the United States.

Confronted by our strong indication in writing, Virgin Records' attorney replies ten days later, simply saying there will not be any decision before further discussion within EMI

Records.

Legal Action in Homeland

The waiting is restless. we ruminate over the possible settlement outcome at the other side of the Pacific. At the same time, there are legal actions we have to tackle on our own big island as well.

It is July 18 that I represent Mr. and Mrs. Duana in sending an attorney's letter to China Television Company ("CTV") and TVBS News Channel ("TVBS") indicating the instances of unauthorized use of Mr. and Mrs. Duana's work.

My letter says. "Without Mr. and Mrs. Duana's permission, the Maison des Cultures du Monde produced the CD containing 'Elders Drinking Song' by Mr. and Mrs. Duana, and licensed the music to the German band Enigma as another unauthorized use in the song "Return to Innocence" on the album "The Cross of Changes.""

Neither of these two albums ever mentions anything about the actual singers. Let alone putting their names on the titles. Of course, it goes without saying that Mr. and Mrs. Duana have never been paid for any royalties.

That "Return to Innocence" is used by the 1996 Atlanta Summer Olympics as their promotion music is another recent instance of unauthorized use of Mr. and Mrs. Duana's work. All of the said instances constitute infringements of the moral

rights and proprietary rights of Mr. and Mrs. Duana.

Therefore, without the licensing of Mr. and Mrs. Duana, playing "Elders Drinking Song" in the Olympics Special Report during the evening news on TV is likely to constitute an infringement as well. We demand that you immediately present anything proving to have a legitimate license, otherwise you should clarify the above points regarding the infringement matters."

It is ten days later that a manager representing CTV comes to my law firm to discuss a possible settlement, hoping that both parties can sign a settlement agreement and a licensing agreement for using "Elders Drinking Song." On top of that, CTV is willing to create a special report about Mr. and Mrs. Duana.

I pass these settlement terms to Rock Records right away, having their General manager explain the deal to Mr. and Mrs. Duana that CTV, one of the infringers, is able to make a public apology and admit who owns the copyright in "Elders Drinking Song." Without doubt, this is a good deal.

We should definitely grab this chance to get Mr. and Mrs. Duana names written down as the copyright holder on at least one official document piece of paper, which will stand us in good stead for our future case, especially now at sight no progress is made in regard to the negotiation with the US companies.

Missed Opportunities

We have no idea why it would take Mr. and Mrs. Duana and their family such a long time to ponder upon the settlement with CTV. They did not agree on the deal until August 8; however, it was too late. As the Atlanta Olympics was ended at that time already, CTV found no benefit from proceeding with any of the earlier offers. It is such a pity, and we have nothing to say but shift our focus to a possible better deal with the other TV station, TVBS.

It didn't go smoothly with TVBS, either. On August 19, the written response of TVBS' attorney is again to our disappointment.

"We learned that the Olympics is duly authorized to use 'Elders Drinking Song' in their promotion song, so our conduct in using the music has nothing to do with the alleged copyright infringement. If Mr. and Mrs. Duanathey claim that they are the copyright owner of 'Elders Drinking Song,' they should prove the ownership of the copyrights."

Obviously, TVBS does not believe that Mr. and Mrs. Duana are the copyright holders of "Elders Drinking Song."

The entire world cannot deny the voice of Mr. and Mrs. Duana exists in the song, but that is another story when it comes to entitlement. As before the law people operate under the legal constraints, it takes all types of evidence to prove

ownership and protect your legal right.

And These are the rules of the civilized world, which is beyond an innocent indigenous man's imagination.

If it were not for Mr. and Mrs. Duana's contract with the record company and the engagement of a team of lawyers, no one would know that the voice of Amis people of Taiwan counts for 50% of the theme song in an album ranked in the Billboard top 100 for 32 weeks and sold over 5 million copies worldwide.

Despite the collaboration between Taiwanese and American lawyers working on the infringement claim, the situation remains unfavorable. Frankly, the voice in the CD is the only proof that can be verified through audio forensics. Lacking the witnesses, documentary and physical evidence to support Mr. and Mrs. Duana as the copyright owner of "Elders Drinking Song," no wonder the domestic and foreign infringers all regard their conduct as authorized use and refuse any settlement.

Here is another example of missed opportunity with the Olympics.

It was said that when Wu Ching-kuo, the member of the International Olympic Committee ("IOC"), reported to the committee that the promotional song of the Atlanta Olympics was sung by Mr. and Mrs. Duana, Juan Antonio Samaranch, the chairman of the IOC, quickly made an instruction on July 17 that the IOC should send an official letter of appreciation to the

singer couple.

However, on the next day the IOC received the letter of an infringement notice from our American counsel representing Mr. and Mrs. Duana, the IOC changed its attitude, stating that no further comment would be made until the end of all legal procedures.

It's not hard to guess that the IOC doesn't want to get involved in a legal dispute. In their understanding, before broadcasting the promotional song, IOC already acquired licensing from the music publisher EMI Records, so how can they be accused of "copyright infringement" afterwards? Facing our lawyer's infringement notice, it is out of the question that IOC will ask EMI Records, the licensor, to give an explanation. Hence, whether the case can go for settlement really depends on the attitude and position of EMI Records.

A Big No, Loud and Proud

Being rejected by the domestic infringers, CTV and TVBS, and facing the IOC's changed attitude, we are eager to know how EMI's attorney will reply. With back and forth communication and explanation from the end of July, mid-August to early September, the other side's attorney stopped communicating with us with one simple excuse of "awaiting a further discussion with EMI Record."

Then another one month passed since the last contact in

September. On October 3, we requested our American counsel to dial a direct phone call to EMI Records, the publisher in the UK. Over the phone, EMI Records promised that the German company Mambo Musik would instruct its attorney to give us a reply within one week. Again, it was an empty promise. On October 8, our American counsel again urged Virgin Records' attorney to reply as early as possible.

So it is the Thanksgiving Eve that the we receive the "final answer."

A big "No". Said loud and proud.

They deny any infringement, and according to the attorney representing EMI Records, they also strongly believe that it would be financially impossible for Difang Duana, who comes from the impoverished Indigenous tribe, to file a copyright infringement lawsuit that might cost up to US$1 million.

We are speechless to such an answer that we have been keen to know for four months. After the four months of waiting in patience, the other party's response to our findings of their copyright infringement turns out not only a rejection to settlement but also words with arrogant contempt. What a slap in the face.

Of course, the disappointment of Difang Duana is beyond description after he learned about this. He cannot understand why the infringers can sit stone-cold, turn a blind eye to the wrongdoings, and ignore how to make the wrong right.

He has never set foot in a court, and he never needs a lawyer. He cannot possibly know that many people who make mistakes will not admit the mistakes until the last minute they realize there might be an unfavorable outcome through the legal process.

In his belief, a mistake will be corrected once found.

It has been four months since the outbreak of the infringement case. We have been trying to settle by sending the warning notice and initiating the negotiations. Now anyone can see the settlement offer get rejected.

As we discuss and analyze in great details, it is clear that Rock Records and Magic Stone Music are in a dilemma: to sue or not to sue.

Once again, I find myself sitting in the meeting with everyone, including Difang Duana, Tuan Chung-tan (Head of Magic Stone Music) and Landy (Pei-jen Chang, the president of Magic Stone Music), evaluating the US litigation and what the cost will be - the time, money, and manpower.

The central role in this case, Mr. Duana, becomes silent. Unbeknownst to him, how much it is going to cost behind the pursuit of justice.

At All Costs

In Difang Duana's eyes and voice, Magic Stone Music sees his longing and feels his persistence for justice. All the

meetings in the past few days come down to one conclusion: Magic Stone Music will support Difang Duana to take the first step in the legal battle at all costs, considering this is to safeguard Indigenous music and Duana's copyright. Actually, in the bigger picture, not only can this battle defend Mr. and Mrs. Duana's interests, but also change Taiwan's image and preserve Ami's culture and dignity.

With the hope of winning a grand legal war against the multinational record label, Magic Stone Music is going to file a copyright infringement lawsuit in the US court.

In the next move, we will decide where to deploy the location, who to be our trial attorney, which court to bring the case to, and how we should claim the damages resulting from the copyright infringement.

Here in Taiwan, what I can do first is gather as much information as I can. After the Christmas holidays end, I fly to the US, contacting a number of law firms to learn the details regarding the litigation proceedings of infringements case.

According to our legal counsels in the US, if Mr. and Mrs. Duana file a copyright infringement case through "summary proceedings," it will only take three months for documentary examination by the court without going through a lengthy trial with a jury, and the total cost would be around US$260,000. However, the chance of winning the case this way would be lower considering it is unclear whether Professor X, the key

person of this case, will be standing on our side or not.

Judging from EMI Records' complete denial of Duana's copyright of "Elders Drinking Song," choosing a summary proceeding is very unlikely to achieve victory in the case.

A "jury trial" is the other option. As a trial is expected to go through a jury, it probably will take about three years, and attorney's fees might be up to US$850,000. This is how expensive and time-consuming a trial by jury is. Considering Difang Duana's age and physical condition, his appearance in a US court or press conference in the US may be too challenging. In fact, even with a victory, there will be very little left in the recovery after deducting the cost to litigate the case through a trial.

Now we know the cons, and let's talk about the pros.

This will be an unprecedented lawsuit, and it will also be such a huge topic that it throws the spotlight on Indigenous music. And let's not forget, a favorable verdict will not only defend Duana's interests but also call for the losing party to pay us the legal fees and attorneys' fees at the conclusion of the litigation, and such fee award would reduce big time to our costs.

VI
Justice Doesn't Come Cheap

Back to Taiwan, these evaluated components and information for assessments triggered a heated discussion within Rock Records. Although everyone is voting for "a jury trial," no one can deny that the total costs are excessively high:

US$1,000 for filing fee, US$3,000 for the deposition of each witness, US$5,000 to US$20,000 for the testimony of each expert (e.g., to retain an accountant for calculating the album revenues or an audio forensics expert for infringing songs), plus the expenses for interpreters and translators, the trips, the mails, the phone calls, the copying costs and other miscellaneous items.

Any of the costs and expenses are going to be out of the pocket of Rock Records, not Mr. Duana, who cannot possibly afford anything what is mentioned here. It is such a struggle. The Head of Rock Records decides to seek other fee arrangement and asks me to see if some American law firms

will accept a combination of fee structure based on stages, say, they first bill for a lower amount as an advanced payment about US$20,000 to 50,000, and they can take the contingent fee - a percentage of the final settlement or awards from the judgment if we win.

It turns out that the majority of American law firms I get in touch with decline to represent us in our case due to the complexity of case nature.

The infringement takes place across three continents - Asia (Taiwan), Europe (France), and the Americas (USA), and the time that the song has been used and the case history span for 30 years (1966 - 1996). Undoubtedly, it is not a walk in the park to explain different versions and amendments of copyright laws of different countries, and then put all the facts together in this case. On top of that, considering the obviously unmatchable status between the opposing party - EMI Records, it is not hard to understand why these law firms are not planning to take our case - the odds of winning our case and getting the contingency fee are incredibly low.

In the course of searching for the representing law firm, I have a Chinese American attorney remind me that the first thing we need to decide is which court to bring this case to, then based on this choice of forum, we choose the suitable law firm. Because it would be inappropriate to engage a law firm located in the West Coast for a case filed on the East Coast.

Similarly, when filing the case in Los Angeles, it would be inappropriate to hire a lawyer from New York. Otherwise, besides the unnecessary bills for transportation, an attorney who is unfamiliar with the customs and procedures of the local court is likely to jeopardize our case.

Look for the Right Court, the Right Jury, and the Right Lawyer

Feeling grateful for the Chinese-American attorney's kind reminder, I decide to take my chance to know further about how to choose the forum. Without growing tired, he continues his analysis:

"EMI Records and the IOC are the defendants in this copyright infringement case. As EMI Records sold the album containing the song "Elders Drinking Song" across the US, you can file the case in any US state. However, considering the plaintiff is a Taiwanese national of Indigenous ethnicity, if the case is filed in a comparatively conservative state or a state with higher percentages of white Americans, such as New York, Boston, and Washington in the East Coast, it is likely the jurors, and the judge have less sympathy for your side and have less understanding toward Difang Duana.

In contrast, it probably will be better to file this kind of international copyright infringement case in the state where more immigrants live and a better-developed entertainment

industry exists, as people there tend to be more open-minded. Say, California is a good place to consider. Its film industry is thriving, and its courts are more familiar with the music industry. More foreign residents there, more chances some immigrants are included in the jury pool. So to speak, the more sympathy you get, the closer you are to winning."

This totally makes sense to me, and I cannot agree with him more! Naturally, I also ask him a favor to recommend some law firms in Los Angeles to us. This Chinese-American counsel quickly recommends me a law firm with which he collaborated before. He says he was impressed with this law firm's brilliant lawyers in handling intellectual property disputes.

Shortly after the conversation, I contacted this new law firm, and after several attempts, they agreed with the terms for lower advanced payment and the contingency fee. Not long after that, they presented us a litigation schedule for the case:

Litigation Schedule

(I) Before January 31, 1997, Mr. and Mrs. Duana should file the complaint in United States District Court for the Central District of California Western Division.

*Plaintiffs: Difang Duana and Igay Duana

*Defendants: EMI Records Ltd., Atlanta Committee for the Olympic Games (ACOG)

(Enigma, Virgin Records, Mambo Musik, and the Maison

des Cultures Du Monde ("MCM") later become co-defendants of the case based on their connections with EMI Records)

*Prayer for relief:

(1) Defendants should pay Plaintiffs reasonable damages that Plaintiffs have sustained. (Such damages are unclear at the pleading phase. During the proceedings, the attorney will have to demand the EMI Records' financial department to provide a full accounting to an independent accountant who is retained by Plaintiff.)

(2) Defendant should pay Plaintiffs reasonable royalties in the future.

(3) Defendants should list Plaintiffs' names on Defendants' products and materials contained Plaintiffs' copyrighted works.

(II) The defendants, EMI Records and ACOG, will have to file their answers with the court in response to plaintiffs' complaint.

(III) The US district court will request the plaintiffs and defendants to exchange the relevant documents and information within 60 days of filing of the complaint (e.g., the licensing agreement between the MCM and Enigma, the publishing agreement between Virgin Records and EMI Records, and the royalty statement reports of EMI Records).

(IV) The court will allow the parties to engage in discovery. Plaintiffs and Defendants can take the depositions to question

the witnesses. EMI Records may request the Plaintiffs, Difang Duana and Igay Duana, and the relevant witnesses to testify in the US.

(V) The court will order a Mandatory Settlement Conference. If a settlement cannot be reached, the case will proceed to a trial, where oral arguments and jury hearings will take place, and end with a jury's decision.

According to the American counsels, the estimated timeframe of legal actions from (I) to (V) is three years. After careful consideration, Rock Records decided to retain this law firm to initiate the case in the California federal district court.

Tasks After Tasks

I thought retaining the American counsels to take over and file the case would cut a lot of my workload in the legal support in Taiwan. But it was just an illusion. I was wrong. In fact, it's the opposite; more work is piling up for me.

Before anyone is filing a copyright infringement case in the US, that person needs to register his or her copyright with US Copyright Office first. And the submission of copyright registration requires translation work for basic information of "Elders Drinking Song" and the records related to Difang Duana's performance. In fact, by the time the registration is completed, we have already spent nearly six months on its

process.

Additionally, our American counsels task me to do research and conclude the legislative history and the revision made in every version of the amendment of Taiwan's Copyright Act since 1966, so the applicable Taiwan's Copyright Act can be identified at the corresponding time point of each critical year in the case:

1966, Professor X collected the recording during the fieldwork;

1979, the song was recorded at First Record;

1988, the live performance was recorded at MCM;

1993, the album was released by EMI Records;

1996, the song was used by the Atlanta Olympics.

Especially, to support the legal basis of the infringed copyright in song's arrangements and the work of performance, I need to focus on legal grounds as well as legal opinions issued by competent Taiwanese authority over copyright laws. So when I print out all my hard work, I get a very thick and heavy legal opinion book, which is comprised of extracts from relevant records and materials of Taiwanese Legislative Yuan along with my analysis and explanations.

However, our American counsels do not find my legal opinions strong enough to support that Difang Duana is the copyright holder of the music arrangement.

"To what extent can the evidence make the judge believe that

Difang Duana re-arranged "Elders Drinking Song?" I ask.

As I get the answer from our American counsels, my mouth is hanging open in shock. The method of evidence they request is nearly impossible to me. Frankly speaking, I just want to quit!

Here is what our American counsel says.

"Lawyer Huang, could you please find the decades-ago version of the song before Duana made the arrangement to it? So we can compare the original version and Duana's arranged version, and show the judge if over 80% of the original song has been arranged or adapted."

And there is more.

"Before presenting the original work and the arrangement to the court, you need to secure the opinion of a Taiwanese expert witness in verifying the differences between the two versions. On top of that, we need to attach one independent English legal opinion on the applicable Taiwan's Copyright Act for reference as well. Independence means neither of us should be writing this legal opinion because the judge will rely on an independent opinion from a third-party expert. As we both represent Difang Duana, we don't have enough credits on such opinion for the judge or for the jury."

A Great Song-Searching Team

The song version before Duana made the arrangement?

Wow! That was a long time ago! How can we discover such an early version of "Elders Drinking Song" made decades ago? How can we have the original melody of "Elders Drinking Song" passed through the tribe for generations?

Tribal elders and Difang Duana once mentioned the folk tale and hummed a small part of the melody in front of us. That is all the clue I have, seriously. I feel this time I've got an impossible mission, and I feel enormous pressure landing on my shoulder. With that being said, I am still the one who takes over this hot potato.

But I can ask for help. Rock Records is the first one on my list.

At my request, Magic Stone staff first dove into the historical files. Then, with their passionate search efforts, they flied to the southeast coast of Taiwan, Taitung, the home of Difang Duana, to get more information.

Understanding the mission's purpose, Duana's Tribe people felt huge motivation; they mobilized entire tribe to look for the source. People were asking and searching around, from interviewing elderly people to overturning the trunks and boxes, even dusting their little notebooks in the house. In other words, we have a most warm-hearted song-searching team out there in the most remote place on the island.

Amazingly, an earlier version of "Elders Drinking Song" was found, and in that earlier time, this song was called "Sakatusa'

ku'edaway a radiw" (lit. "The Second Long Song").

After comparing "Sakatusa' ku'edaway a radiw" with "Elders Drinking Song" arranged by Difang Duana, we confirm that the changes in the arrangement are over 80%, which really can prove that Difang Duana is entitled to own the copyright in the song arrangement.

Our Expert Witness Professor

While our American counsels are pleased to learn our findings, they still point out that the comparison result cannot be made by us. It is better to engage one expert witness to conduct the comparison and analysis, and conclude the result in a written report.

What kind of expert will be qualified for this job? Although anyone can identify the difference in the melody at once, examining the changes in Taiwan's copyright laws in the legislative history of thirty years is not a job for everyone. It is a job for a legal scholar.

I have a perfect candidate in the law school where I graduated from. My senior classmate at the Graduate Institute of Law of National Taiwan University ("NTU"), Ming-Yan Shieh, who became a professor at our alma mater after earning his Doctor of Laws in Germany. Specializing in intellectual property rights law, he has a long list of academic and publishing credits.

Once our American counsels received my fax paper

describing Professor Shieh's expertise and credentials, they found him reliable and agreed with me to engage Professor Shieh as a qualified expert witness. Therefore, we retain Professor Shieh to draft the expert opinion as part of the preparation for filing the copyright infringement case.

The prepared materials for my visit to Professor Hsieh at the NTU Department of Law include case relevant records, statement of facts, my analysis, the old version of the song before arrangement by Difang Duana, together with three CDs infringing Mr. Duana's copyright:

CD No.1. "Amis Folk Song", released by First Record in 1979

CD No.2. "Polyphonies Vocales Des Aborigenes De Taiwan", recorded in 1988 and released in 1989 by the Maison des Cultures du Monde

CD No.3. "The Cross of Changes", released by EMI Records in 1993

Prior to our meeting, I've walked Professor Hsieh through the outline of the case over the phone. So, Professor Hsieh already fully grasped the background and main points before the meeting. When we sat in the faculty common room to compare the two versions, we repeatedly played the new version and the old version of "Elders Drinking Song". After listening for couples of times, Professor Hsieh confirmed that Difang Duana's new version indeed changed over 80% from

the melody of the old version.

Then we began the discussion over the elements in the infringement claims in Taiwan, the US, and France, and whether EMI Records and the IOC should be held liable for infringement. After we reached the agreement and confirmation on the defendant's liabilities, Professor Hsieh accepted the assignment with pleasure and promises to deliver his legal opinions in Chinese and English within one month.

VII
Let's File Our Complaint

Now I have the proper pleading documents ready. With the assistance from Rock Records / Magic Stone Music and my arrangement, Mr. and Mrs. Duana authorize the American counsel to file the complaint to US District Court for the Central District of California ("CDCA").

On the front page of the complaint, it states:

Plaintiffs: Difang Duana and Igay Duana

Defendants: Virgin Schallplatten GmbH, Mambo Musik, Charisma Records of America, Capital-EMI Music, Inc., "Enigma"(the band), Michael Cretu (the producer of the album "The Cross of Changes"), and the International Olympic Committee ("IOC").

Case number is 97-9602 JSL(AIJX).

Complaint for Copyright Infringement.

DEMAND FOR JURY TRIAL.

And here are the summaries of the complaint:

1. This is a civil action seeking damages for copyright infringement under the Copyright Act 1976 of the United

States, 17 U.S.C. § 101, et seq.

2. The Court has original and supplemental subject matter jurisdiction over copyright claims under state law under 28 U.S.C. § 1331 and 1338(a)(b).

3. Plaintiffs, Difang Duana and Igay Duana, are husband and wife. They are the authors, performers, and producers of their musical work recorded in Kupei Road, Taitung City, Taiwan Province, Republic of China.

4. The Plaintiffs claimed that after December 1992, the Defendants respectively, directly and knowingly infringed the copyright in Plaintiffs' musical work by means of copying, public performance, production, distribution or licensing the recording of Plaintiffs' musical work, or taking participation and giving support in the said infringement acts, or profiting wholly and partially from the use of Plaintiffs' musical work in the song "Return to Innocence" by Defendant Michael Cretu and Enigma.

5. The song "Return to Innocence" is collected as a single track on the album "Cross of Changes album."

6. The Defendants Michael Cretu, Enigma, and Mambo Musik participated in and facilitated the reproduction of Plaintiffs' musical work, which brought about the creation and recording of "Return to Innocence".

7. The Defendants Mambo Musik, Charisma Records of America, Capital-EMI Music, Inc., and Virgin Schallplatten GmbH facilitated and participated in the mechanical production and distribution of "Return to Innocence" in the US and throughout the world.

8. The Defendants Michael Cretu and Enigma facilitated and participated in the public performance of "Return to Innocence" by Enigma.

9. The IOC specifically used the Plaintiffs' musical work in the promotional video of 1996 Atlanta Olympics.

10. Defendants' infringing acts directly violated Plaintiffs' copyrights under international laws were unknown to Plaintiffs until 1995.

11. In the booklets inserted in the related audio publications, Defendants failed to explain the source and the authorship of the Plaintiffs' musical work; instead, Defendants established a wrong impression in relation to the source of Plaintiffs' song and recordings.

12. Plaintiffs never receive compensation to which Plaintiffs are rightly entitled. The wrong description in the above-mentioned booklet has caused and is causing irreparable harm to Plaintiffs. Accordingly, Plaintiffs make requests as follows:

(1) All Defendants, together with their agents, employees,

and representatives, should be preliminarily and permanently enjoined from violating the Plaintiffs' copyright in any form of the sale, production, distribution and licensing of the recording of "Return to Innocence" made by Michael Cretu and Enigma, or taking participation and giving support in the said infringement acts.

(2) Defendants should be required to provide a full accounting for all profits, revenues and interests derived from their infringing use of Plaintiffs' musical work; Defendants should also be ordered to pay Plaintiffs all damages that Plaintiffs have sustained as a result of the acts complained of herein, or the amount Court may deem proper under copyright laws.

(3) Defendants should be ordered, before a trial court's decision is made, to deliver all infringing copies, recordings, and audio recordings together with all metal plates, molds, and moldings and any other tools which can be used to manufacture the above-mentioned infringing copies, recordings, and audio recordings, all of which should be impounded and destroyed.

(4) Defendants should be ordered to pay Plaintiff's fees and costs incurred in connection to this matter, including reasonable attorney fees.

(5) Plaintiffs should be awarded any rest of the damages and future damages.

Opposing Parties, Get Prepared!

The war drums began to roar. Indigenous Taiwanese people are declaring war on multinational record companies. It is time for the US court of law to handle this transnational copyright infringement case. After accepting this case, the California court requested the plaintiffs to send one copy of the complaint to each defendant, including EMI Records, Virgin Records, Mambo Musik, the producer Michael Cretu, the band Enigma, and the IOC.

Ten days after filing of the complaint., the presiding judge, J. Spencer Letts, notified Plaintiffs and Defendants that he is in charge of the copyright infringement case of "Elders Drinking Song." Defendants are requested to file an answer within 30 days after service of the complaint, followed by a non-compulsory and informal meeting in the law firm attended by the two parties' attorneys, where they can discuss the preparations for the trial in this case.

The US system of justice is very different from Taiwan's court practice. Take the serving the complaint for example, when a civil suit is filed in Taiwan, besides the original copy of the complaint submitted to the court, based on the number of defendants, the plaintiff only needs to provide the same number of copies to the court's mailroom to complete the process of serving. The plaintiff then simply needs to wait

for the following court notice because it is the court's full responsibility to deliver the complaint to each defendant. If the court fails to serve the defendants at the addresses provided by the plaintiff, the judge will notify the plaintiff to report other addresses of the defendant's household or business operation, or the court can resort to the public announcement in lieu of delivery.

In the US, it is the plaintiff's responsibility to serve each defendant with the complaint and provide a record of the service. Suppose disputes over the process of service arise between the parties, then the plaintiff needs to provide the process server's testimony or evidence to fulfill his or her obligation in service of the process.

Serving all defendants is the first problem our attorneys encounter in the litigation procedure of the case. For those defendants in the form of business entity like the IOC, EMI Records, Virgin Records, Mambo Musik, Charisma Records of America, and Enigma, it only takes some paperwork to serve them with complaints - that is easy.

In contrast, the album producer, Michael Cretu, was not living in his residential premises, which caused problems for the process server to serve him. Having no other choice, our American counsels hired a detective with our consent to track down Cretu's current residence. Only then did we learn that Cretu had been on a personal and business trip to

a Mediterranean island for the past few months, irregularly coming and going, which took lots of effort for the detective to locate him and deliver the complaint to him in person on that Mediterranean island.

Completing a mission like that doesn't come cheap. Needless to say, our party has to pay for all the bills including the detective's charges and his transportation expenses - his airplane and ship to the Mediterranean island.

Along with the case development, these sorts of "surprising" bills just keep coming up, and all Rock Records can do is grit their teeth and pick up the check.

The defendant EMI Records received the complaint on January 20, 1998. On February 9, their retained attorney, Joel McCabe Smith, sent a letter notifying Emil C. Chang (our attorney representing Mr. and Mrs. Duana in the US) of his representation of the defendant in this case. In the letter, he stated that they would respond with the answer to the complaint on February 19, and he made inquiry about the status of service on other defendants, namely EMI and Virgin Records.

Our attorney Chang replied on February 12, reminding the opposing counsel that this case is drawing international attention and the negative comments will come after another along with the development of the litigation. Which means, go get prepared, the defendants and their lawyers!

Filing Lawsuit in France?

Besides representing Mr. and Mrs. Duana in the copyright infringement litigation, Lawyer Chang also sent a "Notice of Dispute" to the American Society of Composers Authors and Publishers ("ASCAP") requiring ASCAP to provide the particulars of the royalties payable based on "Return to Innocence," the infringing song.

Moreover, considering that Mr. and Mrs. Duana may also file a lawsuit against the Maison des Cultures du Monde ("MCM") and other companies involved in the publishing of "Return to Innocence," Lawyer Chang also gets in touch with another collaborative law firm in France. The French lawyer, Therese de Saint Palle, therefore undertakes to carry out some evaluation and research work for us, including the feasibility of filing our case in France, the details of the organizational nature, MCM's founding date and founding purpose, and its source of funds.

French Lawyer Palle listed a series of questions after reviewing our case, and our Lawyer Chang sent her the following response on February 19:

1. Mr. and Mrs. Duana did not know anything about the album made by Professor X or the CD produced by MCM, nor did they give permission in any form, either orally or in writing, for the recordings to be published by the other defendants.

2. In addition to MCM, we also intend to file lawsuits against

EMI, Capitol, and Virgin in France.

3. We have already requested a Taiwanese lawyer to consider bringing the lawsuit against EMI in Taiwan or sending them an attorney's letter. Our intention is to initiate the litigation on a global scale at the same time in order to settle this case smoothly as early as possible.

Lawyer Chang also answered the questions asked by Alexandra, the assistant of Lawyer Palle:

1. The recording made in 1978 has poor quality, and that is why Professor X recorded Mr. and Mrs. Duana singing their song again in 1979. What MCM used for their album was the recording made in 1979.

2. The recordings mentioned above were made by Professor X, who might have acted on behalf of X Art Foundation. The recording of the infringed song "Elders Drinking Song" has never been in our possession.

3. Based on the investigation over the past 18 months, we never find that Mr. and Mrs. Duana ever granted any licenses in writing, for which we shall refer to the Taiwanese lawyer with further verification.

4. "Elders Drinking Song" was the only song in dispute in this case, and a copy of the original song will be sent to Alexandra.

At the same time, Judge Letts of the California court also took some action by scheduling a status conference on April 1, 1998, and after receiving the summons, the two opposing attorneys both gave their appearance on that day.

At the beginning of the conference, Judge Letts told off the defendants in a serious tone, "I will never let such a complicated case enter my court to face the trial of a grand jury. You must negotiate for a settlement now." The defendants' attorneys remained silence. After both parties had stated the claims and arguments, the judge instructed them to exchange documents stating the facts and submit relevant records within two weeks to state.

Five days later, our Lawyer Chang stated in the letter to the opposing counsel,

"1. Plaintiffs are open to reasonable settlement terms, and further discussion of the settlement is welcome;

2. It is a misunderstanding about the law that the recording of 'Elders Drinking Song' performed by Mr. and Mrs. Duana in 1979 is not protected under Taiwan's Copyright Act. We suggest you conduct a legal review on the relevant laws;

3. Particularly in light that under Taiwan's Copyright Act, you cannot succeed with your argument that Plaintiffs' copyright has been transferred to Defendants."

Fast Counterattack

Lawyer Smith, who is representing EMI Records, made an immediate response on the same day (April 6). Rather than replying to what Lawyer Chang's pointed in the earlier letter, Lawyer Smith made attacks on Plaintiffs' failure to serve all the defendants and even denied the Court's jurisdiction over this case. This is an attempt to cause the dismissal of our pleading by procedure phase to prevent our case entering the substantive trial. Hostility can be read in his letter:

"I don't see any connections between Defendant Virgin Records and California federal district court in regard to Enigma's "Return to Innocence". Please advise me of the acts or facts based on which Plaintiffs are entitled to file the case against Virgin Records in California."

On April 15, Lawyer Smith sent us another strongly worded letter. First, he complained our attorney failed to provide "facts, documents, and evidence" as per the Judge's instruction within two weeks, which caused the defendants to request an extension of the deadline to file their answer; and second, he emphasized that Mr. and Mrs. Duana have no legal ground to claim they are the copyright holders of "Elders Drinking Song". Moreover, according to their research, there was no protection for sound recordings in Taiwan's laws in that period of time.

The letter from Lawyer Smith is full of threatening words:

"The relevant rules set out very clearly under US copyright laws during the time at occurrence of the case. We will be very grateful if you can find such legal ground stipulated in Taiwanese laws to support the plaintiffs' claim basis! Once you can state all facts and present the evidence requested by Judge Letts, we will respond immediately as instructed by the Court."

Before the end of the letter, Lawyer Smith restated that Virgin Records does not engage in any substantial economic activities in California. Therefore, the California court has no jurisdiction over Virgin Records, and Mr. and Mrs. Duana should not file a lawsuit against Virgin Records.

Arrogance can be read between the lines, and that is really a provocative letter. By bringing up Judge's name, Lawyer Smith is trying to mount pressure on us and squeeze out more information about the case. Upon the receipt of Smith's letter, Lawyer Chang contacted us urgently. After intensive discussion through phone, fax and email without any delay, we reached agreement and had Lawyer Chang send our reply to retort Lawyer Smith on April 23.

At the beginning of our replying letter, we deny the defendants' allegations that law doesn't provide copyright protection to Mr. and Mrs. Duana, as such allegation is untrue and unsupported by facts.

Then we indicate that at the court hearing on April 1, we presented a detailed analysis explaining the large arrangement

in the song "Elders Drinking Song" made by Difang Duana. Anyone can tell at once the difference between Duana's musical work and the old version before his arrangement, and we have expert witnesses to testify as well.

In return, we demand the defendants to present evidence, including witnesses and physical evidence provided that the defendants allege that Duana's musical work is in the public domain.

Having every confidence, Lawyer Chang gives a good comeback:

"We have studied this case for over one year. No evidence shows that 'Elders Drinking Song' performed by Difang Duana falls in the public domain. All evidence we have prepared shows that Difang Duana retains full ownership of the copyright for the song — there is no question about this.

To help you understand Taiwan's Copyright Act, we would like to inform you that the Act was amended in 1964, 1985, 1990, June and July 1992, and 1993.

Although there were limitations on copyright in the 1964 version, after a comprehensive amendment in 1985, the new law can be applied retrospectively. To maintain consistency with the Berne Convention, the scope of protection in Taiwan's Copyright Act has been expanded in accordance with Articles 13, 14, 24, 27, 29, and 31 of Chapter 3.

Therefore, Difang Duan has a valid legal basis under laws to

own the copyright of 'Elders Drinking Song'."

Questions and Answers, Back and Forth

Regarding the jurisdiction over Virgin Records, Lawyer Chang tactfully replies, "Let's discuss this part once you officially represent Virgin Records!" On top of that, the defendants are requested to answer our following questions in writing:

1. The current residential address of the defendant Michael Cretu (the album producer);

2. The relationship between Lawyer Smith and Virgin Records;

3. Amongst the defendants, who else allege that they can own the copyright in "Return to Innocence"?

4. The legal basis supporting the defendant's allegation that "Elders Drinking Song" is in the public domain;

5. The sources of revenue and financial data regarding the sales of "Return to Innocence" in the US and other regions.

Last thing in the letter, Lawyer Chang doesn't forget to remind the defendants that they had better follow the Judge's instructions to provide substantial answers instead of wasting time on the procedural issue - the tricks of delaying the process,

which is not helpful for this case at all!

It only takes Lawyer Smith one week to send us back another highly provocative letter in response to our sharp reply and questions. It seems that the copyright war has already spread outside of the court.

It is April 30 that we receive Lawyer Smith's response. His remark is quite sarcastic. He criticizes Lawyer Chang's letter on April 23 doesn't do anything to clear up the facts in this case and does not help the defendants understand why the performer Difang Duana has copyright in his song at all.

Lawyer Smith says the defendants have a full grasp as to amendments' history and the spirit of Taiwan's Copyright Act, but they see the amendments do not have anything to do with Difang Duana's rights in this case. Therefore, he demands the plaintiffs to answer the following questions in writing:

1. In which year was the alleged recording in this case made?

2. Why did the plaintiffs sing this song and allow the performance to be recorded? What caused them to proceed with this recording?

3. Are there any documents associated with the alleged recording of the plaintiffs' performance?

4. The plaintiffs claim there was a dispute over the recording of the plaintiffs' performance made by the Maison des Cultures du Monde in 1988, is it Plaintiffs' allegation? If so, we (the

defendants) will present sufficient information to clarify.

5. Plaintiffs allege huge differences between the allegedly infringed song and the song "Elders Drinking Song", which has entered the public domain. Please provide sufficient witnesses and physical evidence for our review on this issue.

Lawyer Smith's letter also comes with the request that the plaintiffs should provide sufficient legal basis to back up the claim that Difang Duana owns the copyright of "Elders Drinking Song" under Taiwan's Copyright Act. This is how he mentions:

"As long as the plaintiffs can present the legal basis, the defendants will have no problem denying the allegation with strong evidence. Referring to the issue of the court lacking jurisdiction in this case, the defendants make no attempt to play the game of procedural issue. If necessary, the two parties can clarify this issue back to the court. Virgin Records will be able to determine its legal representation once t plaintiffs' adequate explanation is given."

While anger might be the first reaction toward hostile response from the opposing party, our Lawyer Chang has to admit that such delay tricks are quite common upon litigating with deep pocket corporations like them. Seeing no intention to resolve the infringement further, Lawyer Chang decides to

collect more evidence supporting Virgin Records' engagement in economic activities infringing the plaintiffs' copyright in California to avoid the judge's misunderstanding. We have our explanation submitted to the court on June 15.

It turns out that our explanation letter upset Lawyer Smith, and our Lawyer Chang got severely criticized by him in two days. Basically, Smith is complaining that we gave no answer to the defendants' questions, so he not only copied the questions in his previous letter, but also gave us his conclusion to whatever answers he may get from us:

"Even the alleged recording is under Taiwan's copyright protection, and the copyright in the sound recording should belong to X Art Foundation, not the plaintiffs - there is no legal basis of the suit at all."

Close to the end of the letter, we are being accused of having been avoiding these questions, which has turned the pleadings exchange between the parties to a one-man show of Defendants; therefore, he intends to present this deadlock to the judge showing how unlikely the factual and legal basis could be clarified any further through the written answers, and he is going to ask the court for a judgment on the merits of the case.

Nevertheless, a "last chance" is referred by Lawyer Smith at the same time. He is willing to wait for the plaintiffs' responses to the questions in Defendants' previous letter within ten days. Failure to answer the interrogatories would lead the defendants

to seek court intervention in order to proceed in the case further.

What intrigues us is that one paragraph in Smith's letter introduces "a Last chance for Plaintiffs" as this tone shift seems to be introducing the room for further negotiation and prospective settlement:

"In your pleading dated of June 15, there is an intention for settlement to reduce the judicial resources in official investigation procedures and relieve the defendants from the burden of providing extra information. We find it absurd to respond to the plaintiffs' eagerness to settle! Unless tomorrow is the end of the world, how can we possibly negotiate a settlement with the plaintiffs, who cannot even justify the legal causes of action in the case? This is illogical to us."

"However, if the plaintiffs wish a settlement and provide such a proposal, I will discuss it with the defendants, evaluate the case and then come back with a preliminary thought about it. In case you insist on this alternative, then there is no need to reply to my questions set forth above."

What is that about? What is their vague attitude about? Are the defendants implying a negotiation on settlement? On the surface, it looks like they are playing touch and forcing us to provide more factual evidence, but when we take a second look into this alternative approach, we find this more like a vague proposal for settlement negotiation.

While it is hard to tell if this is another strategy to delay the litigation progress or an actual intention of settlement, we decide to think twice and not jump to a conclusion. Honestly, the situation depends on the court's attitude if this case moves toward a settlement or trial procedures.

The pleadings sought by our attorney on June 15, 1998 ignited the fires of war over "Elders Drinking Song," and a real court battle between the two parties is about to begin.

The judge held a hearing on July 16, requesting both parties to present the list of witnesses and evidence and the summaries of witness' testimony for information exchange for trial preparation. The defendants' attorneys quickly tackled the assignment - they got in touch with their witness, secured their names to be included in the witness list and passed the list to the judge in a very short of time.

Many under-the-table moves were unknown to us until September 4, when we received Lawyer Smith's list, which unveiled how the defendants have operationalized so many adversary strategies. Taking no precautions beforehand, we find this list a huge punch for us.

What shocks us the most is a name in the defendants' witness list - the Taiwanese ethnomusicologist Professor X.

By Professor X's testimony, the defendants are trying to prove that Professor X is the copyright holder of the sound recording of "Elders Drinking Song" as he was the one who

recorded Mr. and Mrs. Duana's performance in Taitung in 1978.

Furthermore, the defendants are trying to establish the allegation: after Mr. and Mrs. Duana performed at the Maison des Cultures du Monde in 1988, X Art Foundation gave MCM the license to use the recording, so X Art Foundation and MCM could jointly publish the CD, "Polyphonies Vocales Des Aborigenes De Taiwan."

Once such defense perspectives are accepted, then all the uses by defendants become legitimate! This means there will be no problem for MCM to license the song to EMI Records, and surely no one can question EMI Records' licensing to the IOC.

In addition, the list also includes some Taiwanese copyright law scholars, the employees in MCM, and CTV reporters. All of them are set to testify that MCM was duly authorized to use Mr. and Mrs. Duana's voice.

And there is one more defense. The defendants allege that such licensing became known to the plaintiffs in 1993, and this lawsuit was not brought into the court till 1997. In other words, they allege that we missed the statute of limitations.

More Defendants

We cannot believe our own eyes at the list of witnesses, especially for the statement signed by Professor X, which is really shocking to us. But in any case, we have no time to waste. I start to work on the response with the management of

Rock Records, and undertake the liaison with Difang Duana, confirming the details of Professor X's recording at the time. So when Lawyer Chang and I exchange our opinions via phone and fax, he also has a faxed copy of my summaries of Duana's statement.

We notice that the defendants are putting so much effort in getting in touch with witnesses from Taiwan, obtaining their consent and collecting their statements. It looks like they are well prepared for this court battle to the end and will not give up easily.

So we decide to prepare for a long-term war of resistance. Besides hiring more lawyers in the US to strengthen the power of our team, on January 11, 1999, we added 17 companies to the list of Defendants of the copyright infringement, including companies sublicensed by EMI Records such as AKA Production, Sony Music, Warlock Records, and some movie companies.

Those new defendants became the target of the second round of the copyright infringement battle because the licensing source from EMI Records is not legitimate, so naturally, without the right to use the plaintiffs' copyrighted work, those sub-licensees have committed infringement as well.

Obviously, putting these heavy-weight companies on the defendant list signals our will to strike back.

Adding new defendants to our lawsuit is helpful to achieve

our strategic goal – we have successfully mounted more pressure on EMI Records to reopening the second round of mediation. Although the mediation is taking place in the US, during the negotiation process, I am staying up late by the phone on the other side of the Pacific Ocean, ready to discuss with our American legal team anytime. With two parties together with the insurance company, the mediation is 6 hours long; however, no deal is reached due to huge differences in settlement amounts between the two parties.

Confirming that the mediation ended without a settlement, we learn that Judge Letts of the CDCA immediately scheduled a trial date of July 13, 1999. He informs the plaintiffs, Mr. and Mrs. Duana, that they need to appear in the court in California for interrogation in front of the jury.

Well, it has been one and a half years since filing the case; despite we know that both the plaintiffs and defendants must give their appearance at court, the last thing we want is to let this elderly couple go through the trial. And now this nightmare is happening.

Now Difang Duana is already 76 years old, and his physical health is not the same as it ever was. Can he manage a long trip from Taiwan to Los Angeles? With all the fatigue from the long flight and transportation, we have no confidence that he can still maintain his usual composure and tell the facts that happened 30 years ago!

Rolling the Snowball

The great pressure of deciding whether Mr and Ms. Duana should show up in the court has been haunting me. I have spent countless nights discussing with our American counsels trying to find the best solution to prevent this elderly couple from suffering the hassle and come up with some good strategy for the entire infringement snowball which is growing bigger and bigger.

What is our next move?

I think hard about this. To be more accurate, I have spent two months thinking hard about this.

However, thinking does not lead us to a better way out; action does. A moment like this, if we don't go forward to fight for a live-or-death confrontation with the other party, we can't win.

I suggest the management of Rock Records: Let's sue the Maison des Cultures du Monde in France.

When the case broke out three years ago, there were many reasons we hesitated to bring the lawsuit in France and chose to litigate in California only. Back then, we just wanted to focus on the litigation in the US, and we were expecting a faster settlement. Dealing with multiple cases amongst parties in multiple countries means more time, more risks, more costs, and more manpower.

Little did we expect that it would turn out to be a long-term war with the defendants in the US court. Noting that they mobilized so much of the resources, including getting a couple of Taiwanese expert witnesses to testify their allegation, I find the condition becoming unfavorable to us, so I conclude that Rock Records' best shot is to start a new legal battle in France, making a last-ditch effort.

VIII
The Ultimatum

Having a lot of communication over the phone, I received Lawyer Chang's gloomy letter on April 19, 1999. He opines about bringing lawsuits in France and recognizes the pros and cons for us to make a decision. In fact, he is urging us to make a quick decision, ASAP, so he and the French attorney can file this case with the French court in May. The clock is ticking.

The strategy is to push EMI Records to discuss a settlement with us by dragging MCM into this infringement dispute and creating more media pressure. Although in my analysis, suing this French organization sounds like a good plan and probably will help us achieve our goal, but new litigation case comes with an unavoidable increase in labor and financial burdens, and this undeniable burden is weighing in the move of Rock Records' management; I totally understand why they hesitate to make such a decision. In the US, or in France, we Taiwanese are completely foreigners, and there is very little we know about their legal system. For anyone, engaging in a lawsuit is already exhausting, let alone being foreign a plaintiff

commencing legal actions in the defendants' home country.

I am not a stone-cold person. I didn't have the heart to rush Rock Records into making the call. So I waited.

It is three days after my proposal that the Rock Records Head comes back to me with a new idea, and I am all ears. He asks me to give our American counsel a task to see if it could get us a chance to settlement for the third time: The ultimatum. Which is, to send an official letter notifying the defendants and MCM that they have one last chance for a settlement; otherwise, new litigation will begin in France.

I tell Lawyer Chang about this new idea, and he has no idea whether this tentative approach can work, but he still wants to meet his clients' requirements. So he gets in touch with EMI Records' Lawyer Smith revealing our next step, and Smith agrees to forward this message without showing much concern. Giving doubt about this tactic, we move to launch another round of media warfare to gain international publicity.

But something unexpected happened. One week later, a dramatic change comes as a complete surprise: EMI extends an olive branch, agreeing to the third round of negotiation.

Really? The ultimatum letter worked. This meeting conveys to us not only surprise but also some hope for a miracle. If we can reach a reasonable settlement, then our elderly couple, Mr. and Mrs. Duana, can save the trouble of flying to California for the jury trial on July 13!

It is almost an impossible mission for both parties to complete the settlement negotiations before the trial on July 13. In a highly tight timeframe, we request our American counsel arrange the time and place for holding this settlement meeting as soon as possible.

However, in case the settlement turns out a dead-end, we are still preparing our plaintiffs for the court appearance as per the judge's instructions. Lawyer Chang suggests we explain and communicate to Difang Duana every dispute and detail we ever encountered in this case, including all the questions our attorneys and the defendants' attorneys might shoot.

The key is ensuring that our plaintiff will testify along the same lines as our established position. No mistakes allowed. Be mindful of the opposing counsels' series of questions designed to exhaust and annoy our plaintiff to produce an outcome unfavorable to us.

I have thrown myself into this case full-heartedly for entire month in May. On one hand, Rock Records and I are turning the settlement terms over our minds, but on the other hand, I have Mr. and Mrs. Duana come to Taipei again to get them ready to present our side of the story in the courtroom.

In short, we are preparing for the worst, and hoping for the best.

Now the main idea of this strategy is to extend the front line mounting the pressure on EMI Records while attracting

international media attention to our case. And these moves are kicking in!

Apparently, EMI Records is having difficulty dealing with the persistent complaints and strong protests from sublicense companies who were sued and served with the complaints from us. With the threat of our bringing litigation against MCM, EMI Records starts to come to the sense that a settlement does not sound so bad: They ask for one more settlement meeting.

Weeks of blood, sweat, and tears spent in the negotiation finally pay back.

It is June of 1999, good news eventually arrives. Under pressure from the ever-growing defendant list, EMI Records agrees to accept our settlement terms. The deal includes monetary compensations, royalty payment, the admission of Mr. and Mrs. Duana being the copyright holders of the music arrangement and the performance of "Elders Drinking Song." And one more thing, EMI will honor this couple with two Platinum records as gratitude for what they have contributed to the music.

Having the settlement in sight, however, Mr. Difang Duana seems to hesitate and fall into a struggle for whether to take the deal or continue this case in court. From a lawyer's standpoint, the final decision should be left for the client, and I can only provide the cons and pros for the trial or the settlement.

Putting a lot of thought into this offer, and having his family meeting discuss over this decision, a couple of days later, Mr. Duana says to my face that he agrees with the settlement terms.

Mr. Duana tells me, he takes the deal because he considers he and his wife will be officially admitted as the "Elders Drinking Song" licensor to EMI, their contributions will be recognized, and they will receive the Platinum records from the American lawyers, who will come to Taiwan on December 8, 1999.

On top of that, in the future release, the CD will be marked that "Return to Innocence" is an adaptation from "Elders Drinking Song," which is arranged by Difang Duana and performed by Mr. and Mrs. Duana, the Amis couple living in Taitung, Taiwan.

Mr. Difang Duana says he has fought for his respect and successfully achieved his goal through litigation. Meanwhile, in the music of the peace-loving Amis people, there is only embracement rather than confrontation. Facing the apology and sincerity from EMI Records, there is no reason for him not to forgive.

On June 8, 1999, in the presence of the president of Magic Stone Music and me, Mr. and Mrs. Duana signed the settlement agreement, ending this three-year international copyright infringement litigation.

Epilogue

This transnational lawsuit prompted Taiwan's lawmakers (the Legislative Yuan, Republic of China) to amend the existing copyright law in 1998 by adding an article protecting "performance" as an independent copyrighted work. This case has also helped put a new law in place: "Protection Act for The Traditional Intellectual Creations of Indigenous Peoples." Moreover, this suit has become the leading intellectual property law case in many law schools.

1996 年 7 月 19 日魔岩唱片二度召開記者會當天照片。

Photos of the second press conference held by Magic Stone Music on July 19, 1996.

圖片提供：滾石國際 Provided by Rock Records

EMI 唱片接受我方條件，承認〈歡樂飲酒歌〉著作權歸郭英男夫婦所有，並於 1999 年 12 月 8 日來台致贈白金唱片予郭英男夫婦。

EMI Records accepted our conditions and admitted that the copyright of "Elders Drinking Song" belongs to Mr. and Mrs. Duana, and on December 8, 1999, EMI came to Taiwan to honor this couple with two Platinum records.

圖片提供：滾石國際 Provided by Rock Records

1979 年第一唱片錄製發行《傳統民歌篇 1》專輯封面及封底。

The front and back cover of "Amis Folk Song / Traditional Folk Songs Chapter 1" album, was released on 1979, recorded, and released by First Record Company.

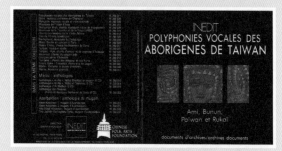

1989 年法國文化之家發行《臺灣原住民複音聲樂》專輯封面及封底。

The front and back cover of "Polyphonies Vocales Des Aborigenes De Taiwan" album, recorded in 1988 and released in 1989 by the Maison des Cultures du Monde.

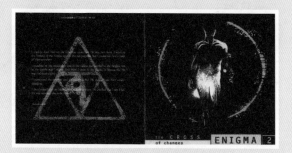

1993 年 EMI 發行謎樂團《徘徊不定》專輯封面及封底。

The front and back cover of Enigma band's " The Cross Of Changes" album, was released on 1993, by EMI Records.

1998 年魔岩唱片發行郭英男《生命之環》唱片專輯，收錄〈歡樂飲酒歌〉。

In 1998, Magic Stone Music released Guo Ying-nan's "Circle of Life" album, which included "Elders Drinking Songs".

圖片提供：滾石國際 Provided by Rock Records

1978 年 8 月 8 日郭英男夫婦於台東市豐谷里，《傳統民歌篇 1》專輯內頁。

On August 8, 1978, Mr. and Mrs. Duana were in Feng-gu-li, Taitung City, resource from the album " Amis Folk Song / Traditional Folk Songs Chapter 1".

台灣台東阿美族馬蘭部落郭英男，Difang Tuwana（1921～2002）。

Guo Ying-nan, Aboriginal people from the Amis Malan tribe in Taitung, Taiwan. Amis' name is Difang Tuwana, was born on 1921 and died on 2002.

圖片提供：滾石國際 Provided by Rock Records